HOW TO ENJOY THE CHRISTIAN LIFE

TWELVE THINGS THIS BOOK CAN DO FOR YOU

1. Add purpose and meaning to your everyday life.
2. Release you from the nagging guilt of past failure.
3. Start you on the highway to balanced, harmonious living.
4. Make the Bible an inspiring handbook for your everyday use.
5. Strangle paralyzing boredom and self-pity: two diseases that may be poisoning your existence.
6. Introduce you personally to God.
7. Unleash hidden powers capable of making you a new person.
8. Make talking with God a normal, enjoyable and life-changing experience for you.
9. Help you test the way of Christ in your own home— before you join a church.
10. Put you on the road to emotional and spiritual maturity.
11. Make you easier to live with!
12. Show you the starting point for building your own faith: the only kind which satisfies and endures.

HOW TO ENJOY THE CHRISTIAN LIFE

by

DON MAINPRIZE

ZONDERVAN PUBLISHING HOUSE
GRAND RAPIDS   MICHIGAN

Printed in the United States of America

ACKNOWLEDGMENTS

Of the chapters in this book the following appeared originally in *Eternity* magazine: "How to Enjoy Talking with God," "How to Enjoy the Bible," and "How to Be Filled with the Spirit." The author is grateful to *Eternity* for permission to reprint.

The author also wishes to thank *The Alliance Witness* for permission to reprint "Time Alone with God."

CONTENTS

HOW TO ENJOY THE CHRISTIAN LIFE

YES, YOU CAN ENJOY

the Christian life. I know that now – but a few years ago when I was a pastor I felt that all the talk I had heard about joyous Christian living was just pious prattle.

Today I thoroughly enjoy my daily experience with the Lord. My faith is real, meaningful and life-changing. But many Christians I know do not enjoy their faith or their God. They admit this – with some embarrassment. Yet many creeds claim that "The chief end of man is to know God and enjoy Him forever."

You may be one who is dissatisfied with the quality and reality of your religious faith. If so, this book was written specifically for you.

Of course, I do not claim to have "arrived." Every Christian and every minister *must* admit with the great Apostle Paul, "Yet, my brothers, I do not consider myself to have 'arrived,' spiritually, nor do I consider myself already perfect. But I keep going on . . . " (Philippians 3:12, Phillips translation).

After a decade of awkwardly groping for God's daily blessing and presence, I am now experiencing a daily renewal

– an intimate, thoroughly enjoyable intercourse with the
Lord, the Self-revealing One.

This book is not the sad and weary account of my groping (Who would want to read that?). Rather it suggests the
guidelines, marks dangerous detours, and tells *how* my appetite for the reality of God has been satisfied for the past
six years. It is not a list of selected, theoretical hunches
on spiritual living.

The guidelines have been followed, pre-tested you might
say, in my own home where true faith and practice meets
its severest test and will, in the final analysis, succeed or
fail. Of course, the ability to practice or adhere to the rules
or guidelines of fruitful, joyful living constitute no fail-safe
guarantee of continuing godliness. When it comes to practicing *daily* what we know, most of us know too much and
practice too little. Christ suggested the necessity of both
doing and *knowing* when He told His disciples in the upper
room, *"If ye know these things, happy are ye if ye do them."*

You will discover that the reality of a spiritual approach
to life and also the joy of Christianity enters our consciousness through practical, everyday experience – and not through
mere adherence to a creed. If we do not practice, that is,
act on what we already know, we dare not expect spiritual
satisfaction. You will personally learn that God is not lost
in an untraceable orbit but is ever present in the life of
each genuine and honest follower of Christ. God is not a
detective, nor a policeman, nor primarily a judge, who hangs
around snooping in our business just enough to make us
uncomfortable.

Believe it or not, God's greatest desire is to befriend us,
to give happiness to us. But you know how it is with last-
ing friendships; they take time, and effort, and two people
(God is a Person; not merely doctrine) who are genuinely
interested in each other. God longs to impart Himself to
you, and with His presence, comes the spiritual and emo-

tional security so needed in our affluent, but spiritually bankrupt society.

True joy will be yours when you consciously and willingly seek God's presence, moment by moment throughout each day. This absorption with God demands no retreat to a monastery; no religious priggishness or other-worldliness. It calls for men and women who will *walk* (keep moving) unflinchingly with God; cultivating His friendship and applying His laws to both their attitudes and actions . . . at home, in the office, and on main street, U. S. A.

The disciples of Jesus lived, walked and talked with their Lord while He was on earth. When He left for heaven the Lord promised to send Someone in His place. On the day of Pentecost the Spirit arrived to begin His ministry. Since that day believers have had the privilege of walking and talking with the Spirit. Since that day the Church has been living in the age of the Spirit.

In our day, and particularly during the past three or four years, there has been a reawakening and restudy of the gifts of the Spirit, particularly the gifts of tongues and healing. This emphasis on the unusual ministries of the Spirit will be a detriment to the Church if it detracts from the normal, everyday ministries of the Spirit and the believer's responsibility to "Be filled with the Spirit," and to "Walk in the Spirit."

The theme of this book is that Christians should be controlled (filled) with or by the Spirit and that this control must be increasingly experienced and extended to bring their entire walk into subjection to the Spirit and the Word. The walk of the believer is herein defined as all of the multiplied roles which he or she is called upon to fulfil.

The joy which is the fruit of the Spirit[1] will be yours when you consciously and voluntarily seek to walk and talk with the Spirit, moment by moment in your everyday life.

This book is written with the prayer that you may consciously experience the Holy Spirit's presence in your everyday life. I would pray with the Apostle, "May the God of hope fill you with joy and peace in your faith, that by the power of the Holy Spirit, your whole life and outlook may be radiant with hope" (Romans 15:13, Phillips).

[1]Galatians 5:22; Romans 14:17; 15:13; Acts 13:52; I Thessalonians 1:6.

1

WHERE IS THE JOY OF THE LORD?

It is woefully obvious that not many Christians speak freely of enjoying the Christian life. They may outwardly appear happy and spiritually content, but inwardly there exists a deep-seated spiritual vacuum, a void that stems from repeated frustrations and spiritual defeats.

Yet we are told that "The chief end of man is to know God and to *enjoy* Him forever." Each year at Christmas we sing "Joy to the World," then tuck that joyous anthem away with the manger scene until the next December.

According to the Bible, Christians can and should be experiencing joy. Our Lord prayed that His disciples might have joy. He prayed, "These things I speak in the world, that they might have my joy fulfilled in themselves" (John 17:13). On the way to Gethsemane He said, "These things have I spoken unto you, that my joy might remain in you, and that your joy might be full" (John 15:11). Thus our Lord, who cannot lie and would not deceive, clearly promised His followers fullness of joy. But what has happened to the joy of the Lord? In our day

The Joyful Christian Is a Misfit

Admittedly there are some joyful Christians who seldom speak of their blessings because of either their temperament or a sort of pseudo-humility. Such a person may receive spiritual refreshment daily but since other Christians in his community apparently aren't so blessed, the joyful Christian feels like a misfit. For him to speak of promises, words of warning, or special guidance that renewed his spirit during his time of meditation, puts him in a class by himself. Other believers, rather than rejoicing in the brother's blessing, tend to categorize him as a spiritual show-off, a Pharisee. Or when the joyful Christian acts on any conviction not generally held by his group, he is met with, "Well, what on earth is wrong with that? Can't a person have any fun?"

The real fun or thrill of Christian living is experienced when a believer translates his own convictions into daily living; transforms his creed into conduct; and senses a definite, regular, if not daily, growth toward godly character.

The Quest for Spiritual Reality

Why do so few believers have a spontaneous, joy-filled walk with the Lord? Since it is true that the chief end of man is to glorify God and enjoy Him forever, why must we admit to the silence of the sad saints? The answer is not simple; it is complex. A pat answer such as, "There is sin in their lives," is not only an inadequate and meaningless generalization, it is worse; it is a horse doctor's analysis of the cancer of the inner man. And to make matters worse, the horse doctor seldom offers a program of spiritual therapy.

Many variable and often invisible factors lead to a defeated Christian experience. Misunderstanding of the nature of the Christian life often leads to discouragement and defeat. Some believers approach Christian living as a naive young teenager anticipates marriage – all pie in the sky. Such an attitude inevitably leads to disillusionment.

Still others suppose that all their problems – of all kinds, emotional, physical, financial, etc. – will vanish because their new Lord, in some magical way, will dissolve them. This misconception leads them into numerous pitfalls, not the least of which is a secret doubt of the faithfulness of God. As the zealous convert sees his own enthusiasm wane, his first love languish, he timidly begins a quest for spiritual reality. Attendance at spiritual life meetings, revival meetings, Bible conferences, and even increased church service form the pattern of frustration. Far too often the result of this quest is added frustrations, a series of spiritual starts and stops. The revival seldom sustains itself. The enthusiasm and blessing, the joy and strength, evaporate in the hot sun of everyday life. Those who possess an extraordinary measure of human persistence will not give up the quest; others refuse to be partners to a seeming deception. They argue, "If this new faith of mine doesn't deliver the goods, I'll drop it. It's the only honest thing to do. Why pretend? Why be a hypocrite?" They quit the visible church.

IS THERE NO SATISFACTION IN JESUS?

This lack of reality in spiritual matters leads the sincere believer into the dismal ditch of self-deprecating introspection and even farther along the highway of doubt. He may well come to doubt his own salvation and question the possibility of ever enjoying the Christian life in an abundant measure. What will happen to such a Christian when the rains come? When adversity strikes in one of its many forms? It will strike, of course! Every person faces adversity some time in his life. Sickness, financial reverses, loss of position, loss of health, or grief from the death of a loved one. These ill winds, blowing on the Christian who has no sense of reality, no witness of the Spirit in his daily life, merely add fuel to the fires of doubt. Even in the absence of adversity this lack of a definite sense of walking with the living God damages, plagues and drains the spiritual nature of the believer.

Often the believer turns to visible supports for his sinking ship of soul. His beloved wife, his dear children, his home, his possessions: these become his ends for living. Having misplaced his affections, he occupies himself with what the immediate present and future holds for himself and his loved ones. This false sense of values leads to further discouragement as far as enjoying the Christian life. His possessions become an ever-present hindrance. And he still finds an emptiness in his spirit: a void which even his loved ones and his tarnishing treasures cannot fill. He learns by experience what Christ meant when He said, "Take heed, and beware of covetousness: for a man's life consisteth not in the abundance of things which he possesseth" (Luke 12:15).

DR. JEKYLL AND MR. HYDE

Those things which the believer once valued highly – the conscious presence of God, the joy of meditation on the Word of God, and fervent, prolonged prayer – are neglected as practices that do not produce satisfaction. What shall the believer do then? Shall he resign as Sunday school teacher? No, faced with the necessity of "looking and acting like a Christian," he decides to play the part. He'd rather be an unhappy professing Christian than an unhappy, profane deserter. He is reluctant to give up the Christian view of man and things; inwardly, perhaps mentally, he is

convinced that these things are so. Yet his experience denies
his faith. No joy and little reality attend his daily pathway.
Unsympathetic observers would condemn and shout, "Hypocrite!" If this is hypocrisy, it is innocent hypocrisy. It is
not selfish pretense; its roots reach deep into the Christian's
inner man. It is a forlorn attempt at spiritual self-preservation.

A FORM OF GODLINESS?

In the public eye and in his church life, he continues
to walk in conformity to the standards, and taboos, and
shibboleths of his church. He can even assert he's glad he
turned to Christ. "My salvation," he argues to himself,
"is the one thing I'm glad about even if I am not bubbling
over with joy." He reads his Bible sporadically, trusting
that God will speak to him. He attends prayer meeting, or at
least Sunday morning church services with the hope that this
slump will magically dissolve. Keep in mind that this false
front originated in an inability to find spiritual reality—
not as a deliberate attempt to deceive. Nevertheless, he must
admit that he maintains a form of godliness but does not
find the power and presence of the God of joy (Psalm 43:4)
in his everyday life.

GLORY OR GRIND?

If we profess Christianity, are we rejoicing in the fullness
of joy our Lord promised? Is there real joy to be found in
our faith in this age of anxiety? Is our Lord's promise and
prayer for our joy, yes, even our fulness of joy, a possibility?
The author, after spending ten years in wilderness wander-
ings, groping for spiritual reality and genuine joy *even while
he was pastoring,* has for the past six years experienced a
deep and abiding, a daily and overflowing walk with the
Lord. Many times he had thought that such an experience
was either impossible or else reserved for a chosen few who

had found some magical formula. Now, out of gratitude to God, he cannot but speak and write for God's people the things which he has seen and heard. *We can* have a walk with the Lord that is vital (living), warm, and filled with *spontaneous* praise and thanksgiving.

But Must We Be Joyful?

In his textbook, *Modern Psychiatry*, William S. Sadler suggests strongly that many people "enjoy poor health." Dare we as Christians "enjoy poor spiritual health" and suffer the disease of joylessness? Why should we enjoy the Christian life? Although the reasons are manifold, one centers on the influence of our joy – or its absence – on our own self-image. Our first love for Christ often fades away; but its memory lingers and we feel that somehow we can regain that plateau of spiritual health. With the failure to do so comes a lingering sense of guilt, the development of an inadequacy image; in short, we become joyless defeatists.

But continued defeat is foreign to the normal Christian life. Surely the Lord grieves when He sees the joylessness of His redeemed people. Because many believers have accepted life in the lowlands and valleys as normal, the church of Christ has been subtly infected with the malady of spiritual mediocrity. As individuals and as a community of believers we have not appropriated the fullness of joy bequeathed to us by Christ. Thus, we are poor examples for our Lord. We must never underestimate the influence of our joyous living on the nonbeliever. If we are walking in the Spirit of love and joy which Christ has provided, we will, in due time, make people thirsty for God.

No One Cause – No One Cure

So now we see the problem. Fullness of joy is our heritage but not our experience. How shall we bring ourselves, or how can we be brought to, the walk of continual communion with Christ as we walk among men? This writer is convinced that God's people can experience daily, intimate, and thoroughly enjoyable communion with God, the Self-Revealing One. Of course *there will be defeats and failures;* they are part of God's program to *gradually* conform us to the image of Christ. That is why each believer must echo the Apostle Paul's evaluation of his spiritual life, "Yet, my brothers, I do not consider myself to have 'arrived' spiritually, nor do I consider myself already perfect. But I keep going on..." (Philippians 3:12, Phillips translation).

Just as there is no one cause for spiritual defeat so there is no single cure or formula which can be guaranteed to unlock the blessing of God on an individual's life. A broad knowledge of the Bible or theology, even a host of degrees, earned or honorary, cannot assure spiritual reality and joy. Evangelicals, as a segment of Christendom, probably know the Bible and its teachings as well as any other group. But knowledge alone is not power – it must be acted on. And when it comes to practicing daily the spiritual principles we know, most of us know much more than we practice. Some Christians suppose their spiritual vitality may be maintained simply by attendance at church meetings. Seeking spiritual life and sustenance dare not be confined solely to church meetings. True, these should be attended. But if we try to maintain a joyful walk with the Spirit on the strength of attendance at church and prayer meetings, we will become weary and faint by the wayside. Something more is needed.

EVERY DWELLING A TEMPLE

God Himself, and strength for the spirit, must be found day by day in the unceremonious, unseen, and unlauded hours spent in our own private meeting place with God. Such trysts, if conducted regularly in the proper spirit and with

Scriptural motives, will saturate us with the presence of
God and help us relate our faith to every area of our daily
lives. Our spiritual vitality and its by-product, spiritual
reality and joy, must be found day by day *in our own homes*
as we pore over God's Word in prolonged, but relaxed,
sessions of prayer, Bible reading, and intense meditation.

Far too often we are guilty of seeking magic formulas that
will guarantee spiritual success and produce Christian character. We want character; but we despise crosses. It is
difficult, if not impossible, to find crosses without *tears,
time,* and *self-discipline.* In our merry-go-round, organization-
centered society it takes Spirit-empowered and -inspired discipline to stop and think; to meditate on God's Word; to
discover personal weaknesses of character; and to erase the
imperfections in our walk before God and men. But our
superficial society no longer sees seeking God as the constant and basic source of happiness, joy, and spiritual vitality. We do not need to be convinced that we must "take
time to be holy –" We simply *must* do it.

Defeat here is defeat in every area of our lives. Although
others may for some time be unaware of our failure to spend
time with God, sooner or later our weakness will show itself.
All too often when we fail to meet the Lord in a vital way
every day – we think He is peeved at us. On the contrary,
He is grieved at our absence at His throne (Jeremiah 2:32).
We know, from the Word of God, and from our own experience, that we should turn to God daily – and that failure
to do so not only weakens our walk with the Lord but it
also amounts to sin. The wise and practical James has told
us clearly... "To him that knoweth to do good, and doeth
it not, to him it is sin" (James 4:17). *And the joy of the
Lord departs when we walk in sin – whether sin of com-
mission or of omission.*

There is joy and adventure in walking with God day by

day. It is the legacy or inheritance of all believers. It can be yours! But how? It starts with your use of time. *Do you have time for God?* If you do, you will find the next chapter helpful. If you do not, you will find it difficult to enjoy the Christian life. But we always have time for the things we consider needful. Is there anything more needful in your life than to spend time alone with God? Remember, such time is *only* the gateway to gladness. In His presence is fulness of joy. He has promised, "Ye shall seek me, and find me, when ye shall search for me *with all your heart*" (Jeremiah 29:13). Why stay in the Valley of Sighs?

2

TIME ALONE WITH GOD:
The Gateway to Gladness

If you will take time daily to wait on the Lord, He will make communing with Him a joyous, life-changing tryst.

Deep within the inner man of every Christian lies a hunger, a thirst, a longing for an intimate relationship with the Living God (Psalms 42:2; 84:2). This longing will not be satisfied by regular church attendance, public prayer meetings, or in fellowship with other believers. Our hearts cry out for spiritual reality.

And at one time, months, or even years ago, our hearts did overflow with the thrill of God's presence. Then something happened. The fervor of our affection died away like embers on frozen ground. In the presence of other believers we maintained all the visible motions and clichés of a spiritually oriented life. We went to church and prayer meetings. But inwardly we fought to keep our spiritual life alive. We tried all the remedies, books on the crucified life, the victorious life, the sanctified life, and so forth. We may have traveled miles to sit at the feet of some spiritual giant, hoping to recapture our lost joy.

We often left such meetings excited, feeling that we had at last rediscovered our lost reality. But within a week or so, the walls of our theoretical castle caved in on us. Sadly we realized that we had not, apparently, discovered the Christian's secret of the joyful, vital walk with the Lord. We were still anemic, powerless, and in a sense – counterfeits. We hated ourselves. We were hypocrites and we knew it.

What can be done to break this recurring pattern of defeat? Can we regain the joy of the Lord? And having regained this strategic ground, how can we hold it against the daily, varied assaults of the enemy? Just what is the Christian's secret of a joyful life?

To start with we must realize again that there is no single secret to a joyful Christian life. No hallowed key unlocks God's storehouse of blessing and makes us automatically "mountain-top" Christians. No magical catalyst exists, no spiritual vaccination is available at the corner church that will make us immune to the peculiar diseases of the spirit, or give us "once-for-all" victory. Such teaching is a dangerous delusion, based on a watered-down view of the heinousness of sin. We must all beware of easy solutions, of seeking some single spring or latch, some *Open sesame!* by which we enter the supposedly enchanted door of joyful, abundant living.

Life is too complex, too many-faceted for one element to be a controlling factor, and the Christian life is no exception. There will be no final battle with the world, the flesh, and the devil in the spiritual warfare of the believer until that day when he lays down his armor and enters the presence of the Lord. The holy war continues as long as there is one enemy, within or without, which seeks to invade and overthrow the throneroom of our hearts.

THE PROCESS OF MATURITY

These spiritual conflicts serve God's purpose and program for our lives. We should always keep before our minds the glorious and gracious truth that God's chief *purpose* for us is, and has always been, that we should glorify Him and enjoy Him forever. God's *program*, however, is to conform us gradually to the image of His Son. He could do it "in a moment, in the twinkling of an eye," but He has chosen the slow, sometimes painful process of growth. Because of our human nature and our failure to turn to God every moment, this maturing process includes setbacks and failures as well as advances and victories. As the writer of Proverbs puts it, "For a just man falleth seven times, and riseth up again..." (Proverbs 24:16). Our spiritual metabolism or growth continues day by day, hour by hour, moment by moment. It is a process in which we can and must participate willingly. It is nothing less than God the Holy Spirit at work in us changing us, restoring us, conforming us to the image of His Son. Scripture verses teaching this daily renewal by the Holy Spirit are II Corinthians 4:16; Titus 3:5; Romans 12:2; Ephesians 4:23; Colossians 3:10.

This daily renewal or growth is a joyous result of walking by the power and under the influence of the Holy Spirit. It will be discussed more fully later in the book.

Instead of speaking of a one-way path to spiritual reality and satisfaction, we may speak of several essentials which we dare not neglect if we hope to grow spiritually toward a harmonious, balanced, and joyful spiritual life. A few of these elements are: the proper use of time, daily self-discipline, meaningful Bible reading, the conscious, moment-by-moment presence of the Holy Spirit, a sensitivity to sin, prolonged and fervent prayer, faithful Christian service, Spirit-led witnessing, and instantaneous and continuous obedience.

"Oh, no!" you groan. "I've heard all of that before. I've tried each of those remedies but I'm still not really *thrilled* about my Christian life. I want something new – I've tested the old ways without success."

You and I do not need some esoteric approach to living the Christian life. We need to practice and to learn to enjoy what we've known for years. We must re-examine and stop neglecting the axioms of spiritual living.

THE PRIORITY OF TIME, DESIRE, AND DISCIPLINE

No Christian dare rephrase another man's theories or techniques when speaking or writing on any phase of spiritual living. Any view of vital Christian living must be experienced in one's everyday life before it can be shared effectively with others. The Lord has taught me some thrilling lessons in fellowship with Him during the past six years; these I would hopefully share with all of God's people everywhere. There is no room for spiritual pride of any sort. As the Apostle Paul reminds us, "For who maketh thee to differ from another? and what hast thou that thou didst not receive? now if thou didst receive it, why dost thou glory, as if thou hadst not received it?" (I Corinthians 4:7). Our desire is simple: we wish to be a "helper of your joy" (II Corinthians 1:24).

The hardest lesson that I had to learn was that a believer *must take time to grow spiritually.* It took me ten years to learn this simple lesson in spiritual conditioning. It is not true that a daily devotional time automatically guarantees spiritual growth. But unless we do set aside (sanctify) a regular time to talk with the Lord and to meditate on His Word we cannot hope to grow toward Christian maturity. Some of us disciples in the school of God learn slowly. My decade in kindergarten was long and dreary for the most part; yet, God was, and still continues to be a faithful and merciful teacher. Sad to say, I began to doubt the goodness of God and the truthfulness of His promises. Even while pastoring a small church I came to feel that the joy of Christianity, the "glad tidings of great joy," of which I had heard so much, was either a lie or an unrealistic exaggeration.

One of my chief problems was that I attempted to come to grips with God in the unlikely scope of ten-twenty minutes a day. Many times I failed to make what I felt was a vital contact with the living God. At times I would be faithful and consistent and every now and then I would sense the breath of the Holy Spirit. Gradually the Lord taught me that I was perfunctorily performing a religious duty. I was trying to harness the Spirit of God to my hurried schedule. In fact, though not in actual words, I was saying, "Well, Lord, here I am again, just as I am supposed to be. Speak now, *right now*, because I must be about my Father's business."

The truth is we cannot hurry God. Neither can we effectively experience the reality of His presence while we have one eye fixed on the clock. When I finally learned that I must take time, much time, to be alone with God, my devotional time became a momentous, anticipated tryst. *It did not become so instantly in some dramatic, earth-shaking experience.* (It has happened that way for many others and this book in no way wishes to detract from either the fact or the reality of such experiences – as long as they result in a walk that pleases God.) In my case it took place gradually over a period of six to eight months as I meditated at length each morning on the book of Proverbs. I believe I strolled slowly through this fruitful garden six times, using four versions and two translations. As I enjoyed my feast daily it came to be a necessary part of my life.

No Natural Appetite for God

One humbling lesson I had to learn was that I did not naturally desire to spend time with God. Nothing in my sinful nature called me to worship the Lord daily. Any desire for communion was, and had to be, both God-inspired and God-empowered. Many times I had no felt desire to seek His face in prayer, reading, or meditation. What does a disciple do when he knows he should take time with the Lord but *he doesn't want to?* The disciples of spiritual honesty and reality would raise up and say: "Forget it. Don't go through the motions if your heart is not in it." Someone else affirms, "Discipline yourself. Do it whether you want to or not. God will honor your effort."

Sometimes such admonitions are apt and helpful. But to spend time regularly with the Lord out of a sense of duty and without a deep desire, leads a person to empty, hypocritical ritualism. How much better to pray as the psalmist did when he faced this lack of desire for God and His Word? He admitted his emptiness and turned to God, praying, "O that my ways were directed to keep thy statutes!" "Incline my heart unto thy testimonies", "My soul melteth for heaviness: strengthen thou me according unto thy word" (Psalms 119:5, 36a, 28). As we honestly and frankly admit our spiritual sluggishness, or coldness, and natural distaste for holy communion and (in the very act of confession and admission) ask God to quicken us, to revitalize us, He will do it – if we are willing to take *enough* time to wait before Him.

Another difficult lesson I had to learn was that being a disciple calls for discipline – daily discipline. As a pastor for five years I found it difficult to form the habit of daily devotions. I often neglected the heavenly altar in favor of visiting the sheep or preparing a "sermon." I knew that

"Habits are strengthened by every repetition and weakened by every exception"; yet I usually scored more exceptions per week than repetitions. As incongruous and discordant as it may sound, I discovered that, at least for me, there was a direct relation between the joy of the Lord in my life and the clang of the alarm in my bedroom.

When we take time to be alone with God is an individual matter hinging upon many varied factors; that we must take time is an inviolable axiom or law of the spiritual world. To break this law can only result in spiritual disorders, and eventually a life of frustrations, defeats and miseries.

Why have many Christians deserted the quiet hour? And why is it such a battle to maintain the habit of personal devotions? One reason believers neglect the practice of private devotion is their past failures to find true satisfaction. Again, how many other believers have they known who not only spend much time alone with God but also share their private experiences with fellow believers? How long since someone has come up to you and said, "Brother, let me share with you the encouragement I received from the Lord this morning"?

Is God a Stranger to You?

An even more tragic reason for not spending time with the Lord is that few believers have taken time enough with Him to learn the joy of His presence, or to sense the power of His Spirit as He transforms their weaknesses into true Christian character. In short, *God is a stranger to many Christians.*

Have you ever been introduced to a stranger, then immediately been left alone with him? Rather awkward, wasn't it? You felt at a loss to make conversation – you didn't know the goals, interests, or character of this new acquaintance. What you needed was either a more extensive introduction or time enough to become more thoroughly

acquainted. The same needs exist in our spiritual relationship with the self-revealing God. As we begin to spend more
time in His presence it will be easier to linger before Him
in unhurried, unembarrassed communion.

We have all determined to spend time with the Lord every
day only to find that in a few days or weeks our determination has languished. Here is the cogent and helpful advice
of Dr. Wilbur M. Smith as given in his book, *Profitable
Bible Study: "Do not let anything defeat you in this most
important part of your Christian life.* It is the secret of
everything!   Defeat here is defeat all along the line! Even
if you do lose a day, start again the next day. Even if . . .
you should lose a whole week, or if your Bible should remain
closed for a month, begin anew now . . . Even if you have
started and failed a dozen times, you can begin again
now . . . ."[1] (Italics his.)

The fact is that every Christian, whether a pastor, a mis-
sionary, a spiritual life speaker, or even your godly grand-
mother, has failed now and then to meet the Lord daily.
Where is our gumption, our determination, our perseverance?
Let us decide that, by God's grace, we will spend time with
Him every day. Why not begin now by giving God at least
a half hour of your day? Plan your time to include reading,
meditation, listening, praise, confession, adoration and petition.
Expect God to speak to your inner man through His Word.
If you will determine to give God enough time and seek
diligently and prayerfully to know and obey Him, He will
reward you, He will manifest Himself to you (John 14:21).
Remember, God "is a rewarder of them that *diligently* seek
Him." As you take time to wait on the Lord daily, He will
make communing with Him a joyous, life-changing experience!

[1]Smith, Wilbur M., *Profitable Bible Study*, W. A. Wilde Company, Boston,
1953, p. 71.

But suppose you have earnestly tried to maintain a time of Bible reading and prayer but have found it lifeless and unenjoyable? What then? Or perhaps you have found it impossible to discipline yourself daily? Where can you find help?

There is Someone whom Jesus sent to be our Helper and constant Companion. Do you know Him personally? He is the Holy Spirit. He is to be our Teacher and to produce love, joy, and self-control in our lives. The Bible commands us to "Be (being kept) filled with the Spirit" (Ephesians 5:18). The Apostle prayed that Christians might "be filled with all the fulness of God" (Ephesians 3:19). We will discuss this filling in the next four chapters.

3

THE FILLING OF THE SPIRIT:
A BIBLICAL REVIEW

" . . . mind . . . the things of the Spirit." Romans 8:5.

After I began enjoying my Christian experience again I started (in my devotions) a prolonged study of the New Testament teaching of the Holy Spirit. A later book will spell out my discoveries in detail.

One of my first observations was that Matthew, Mark, and John have nothing to say about the filling of the Spirit. Almost all we learn from the Word of God about this teaching comes from the pen of Luke. The Apostle Paul refers to the filling specifically in only one sentence.

But let us turn to Luke who, next to John and Paul, has more to say about the Holy Spirit than any other inspired writers.

A study of Luke's references leads us to divide them into three distinct classes. One group refers to the continuing *process* of being filled. Another alludes to a *state* of being filled. And the last includes definite *instances* of persons being filled.

INSTANCES OF ACTUAL FILLINGS

The first person Luke mentions as being filled with the Spirit was Elizabeth, the mother of John the Baptist (Luke 1:41). Her first reaction was to begin speaking. In this case, she praised her cousin Mary.

The second person described as filled with the Spirit was John's father, Zacharias (Luke 1:67). And again we note the same occurrence – he began speaking, praising the Lord God of Israel.

Before passing to the next case, let's back up and examine the lives of this couple. What kind of people were they that God would fill them with His Spirit? Luke gives us this answer, "They were both righteous before God, walking in all the commandments and ordinances of the Lord blameless" (Luke 1:6).

They were not without sin, but by God's grace they longed to obey God and keep His commandments, to depart from evil and to do good. In short, they were clean vessels before God and ready to obey Him. From Genesis to Revelation this is the sort of person God wishes to walk with: believers who are yielded and clean in His sight.

In these cases we see no divine comment on the actual experience of the person; only that those so filled spoke the praises of God. (It seems absurd to me to suppose that those so moved did not identify emotionally with the experience, as if they were mere phonograph records.)

The next major passage on the filling occurs in Acts 2. At this point some synonymous Lukan phrases must be introduced as describing this filling experience. Jesus had told the disciples to wait in Jerusalem until they were "endued with power from on high" (Luke 24:49). In Acts 1:4, 5, Luke quotes Jesus as describing the same event in these words, "...ye shall be *baptized with the Holy Ghost* not many days hence."

Now when that day came, Luke chose to say the disciples "were all filled with the Holy Ghost" (Acts 2:4). Without twisting or arguing with the facts, this strongly asserts that what happened on Pentecost can be described in several different ways. In fact, Luke describes this event in eight different phrases!

Clearly "the filling," "the baptism," and the "enduement" refer to the same event and experience in the lives of the disciples. Now what was this experience like?

It was accompanied by audible and visible phenomenon: "a sound from heaven as of a rushing mighty wind, and it filled all the house where they were sitting. And there appeared unto them cloven tongues like as of fire, and it sat upon each of them."

An emotional experience? Undoubtedly. In addition each believer was filled with the Spirit and began to speak in other languages. The comments of .the observers prove that the Galilean disciples actually spoke in languages other than their own.

The Apostle Peter explains this miraculous event by saying it is a fulfillment of the prophecy of Joel. Undoubtedly the two introductory phrases, "and it shall come to pass" describe the days of the apostles and the present age. Notice (1) It shall come to pass that I will pour out of my Spirit on all flesh, etc. and (2) It shall come to pass that whosoever shall call on the name of the Lord shall be saved. Clearly today is the age of the Spirit's outpouring and the day of salvation.

The next case of the filling or baptism of the Spirit is at another prayer meeting after the disciples, Peter and John, had been released from prison. In this case, a group filling (Acts 4:31), (1) the house was shaken, (2) they were all filled with the Holy Spirit, (3) and they spoke the word of God with boldness.

Notice that these people had already been filled or baptized with the Spirit before, thus illustrating that more than one filling or baptism is Scriptural. See also that the filling had a pronounced effect on their speaking. And finally, this experience would affect the disciples emotionally. Have you ever been praying and had the house shaken? If so, I suggest you would be moved deeply.

The next reference to an instance of filling is Luke's quotation of Ananias' conversation with Saul. He said, " . . . Brother Saul, the Lord . . . hath sent me, that thou mightest receive thy sight, and *be filled with the Holy Ghost"* (Acts 9:17). We assume Paul was then filled.

There are no other incidents in the New Testament where people are said to have been filled with the Spirit.

Persons "Full of the Holy Ghost"

Luke describes some believers as "full of the Holy Spirit," or "being filled with the Spirit." These references lead us to believe that a person could be observed and then described as "full of the Holy Spirit." Some, apparently, stood out from the average run of believers.

The first person described as "full of the Holy Spirit" is our Lord. Of course we know that "God giveth not the Spirit by measure unto Him" (John 3:34). In this state, Jesus was led of the Spirit to the temptation in the wilderness! Obviously the Spirit-filled believer is not immune to temptation.

The second person so described is the Apostle Paul as he stands before Annas, Caiaphas, and other religious leaders. This is a fulfillment of Jesus' promise that the Spirit would speak in believers when they were brought before rulers and kings (Matthew 10:16-20; Mark 13:9-11; Luke 12:11-12).

The next case provides ample evidence that the state of "being full of the Holy Ghost" could be discovered by observers. The apostles told the church to " . . . look ye out among you seven men of honest report, full of the Holy

Ghost, and wisdom . . . and they chose . . . ." (Acts 6:1-5).

Later we see Stephen, one of those chosen, preaching to the hateful Jews. He is described as "being full of the Holy Ghost" and looking straight into heaven at the Lord Jesus (Acts 7:54-56, a clear fulfillment of Acts 2:17e).

Barnabas, the Apostle Paul, and John the Baptist are mentioned as men full of the Holy Spirit (Acts 11:24, 13:9 and Luke 1:15).

The final class of Lukan passages on the filling refers to the

CONTINUING PROCESS OF BEING FILLED

We have seen the same group of believers filled with the Spirit at different times. Two other passages lead us to believe that being filled with the Spirit is to be not only a repeated experience but that it is our personal responsibility to be kept filled.

We read in Acts 13:52 that the disciples "were filled with joy and with the Holy Ghost." The verb in this verse deserves special attention as it is in the imperfect tense. As such, it implies continued or linear action. It could be properly translated "they were being filled with joy and with the Holy Ghost." In other words it was their continuing experience.

This brings us to Paul's verse in Ephesians 5:18. The latter part of this verse could be paraphrased "Keep on being filled with the Spirit." The verb is in the present passive imperative. Thus it constitutes a command and suggests that the situation referred to be continued or repeated. In a later chapter we will try to show how we can obey this command.

As a final comment on the continuing process of being filled, we should note that in each case in the New Testament where the action of a person *being filled* is referred to, the verb *filled* is in the passive voice. Perhaps you are wondering,

"Exactly what does the passive voice mean? And why is this usage so significant?"

The passive voice is defined by A. T. Robertson in these words, "The passive presents the subject as acted upon, receiving the action, rather than doing the action."[1] In other words, we do not (and can not) fill ourselves with the Spirit – God must fill us or we will not be filled.

But what is our part in obeying this clear command? That is discussed fully in a later chapter. At this point let us summarize our findings.

The New Testament relates several instances of individuals and groups being filled with the Holy Spirit. The Pentecost experience can also be called an "enduement" or "the baptism with the Holy Ghost." Believers were baptized with the Spirit after Pentecost. In no instance are the people said to be seeking to be filled, never are they overcoming a supposed divine reluctance to fill them. In two cases the persons are described as "righteous before God," the disciples in each case were at a prayer meeting, and the Apostle Paul was walking in obedience to the light he possessed.

In every instance, this filling influenced the recipient or group to speak, or influenced the character of his or their speaking. A later chapter will point up the significance of this in witnessing.

The New Testament teaches that a person may so live that he can be described as "full of the Holy Spirit." In a later chapter we will set forth some of the characteristics of a Spirit-filled Christian.

The New Testament teaches that believers may be filled again and again with the Spirit on different occasions. Moreover, we are commanded to keep ourselves filled with the

[1]Robertson and Davis, *A New Short Grammar of the Greek Testament,* Haprer and Brothers, New York, 1933, p. 291.

Spirit. In the chapter, "How to Be Filled with the Spirit," we attempt to show the believers' part in this experience.

Paradoxically, we cannot fill ourselves with the Spirit – God fills us. But – several conditions must be met and we, empowered by the Spirit, bear the responsibility to meet these conditions.

4

HOW TO BE "FILLED WITH THE SPIRIT"

" . . . ever be filled and stimulated with the (Holy) Spirit."
Ephesians 5:18.

Are you filled with the Spirit? You ought to know. In fact, you owe it to yourself, to others, and to God to be able to answer "Yes."

If you are filled with the Spirit you'll be a better husband, a better wife, a better parent, or a better single person. Without the filling of the Spirit you cannot hope to please God in all your ways, nor can you really enjoy the Christian life.

The Christian who is filled with the Spirit and walking in the Spirit will be bearing the fruit of the Spirit in his life. That fruit includes joy and temperance (or self-control), elements that will enable us to turn to God daily for sustenance.

The Bible teaches plainly that believers should be filled with the Spirit. The book of Acts tells us that on several occasions the early Christians were filled with the Spirit. The Apostle Paul wrote to the Ephesian church saying, "And be not drunk with wine, wherein is excess; but be filled with the Spirit" (Ephesians 5:18).

But what is the filling of the Spirit? Why is this filling necessary? And how can I be filled with the Spirit?

One fact seems clear: all believers are commanded to be filled with the Spirit. The verb in the Ephesian verse is in the imperative mood; it is a command. It is important that we know what the filling of the Spirit is so we can obey the command.

The filling of the Spirit refers, I believe, to the complete control of the total person by the Spirit of God. The immediate context supplies a contrasting illustration: that of excessive drinking. An intoxicated person is completely controlled by drink; his body, spirit, and mind is saturated with and controlled by drink.

Further evidence supporting this definition may be seen by the use of the Greek word for filling. For example, in Romans 1:29-32, the Apostle describes the unregenerate heart of man as "being *filled with* all unrighteousness." Then he lists fifteen negative attitudes and seven sins of action with which these men are filled or controlled. Other examples may be found in John 16:6 and Acts 5:3.

In contrast with the drunk man whose faculties are dulled and weakened, the Spirit-filled man loses self-control to Spirit-control and his mind and will are sharpened and strengthened in the surrender. Complete control of the believer by God, the Holy Spirit, is the Father's goal for the Christian. It will be true of us in the future when "we shall be like Him" (I John 3:2). Right now the Christian's goal should be to be increasingly controlled by the Spirit in every area of his life and at all times.

Contrary to popular sentiment, the filling of the Spirit does not *necessarily* involve an emotion-packed experience. Neither is such an experience precluded. The fillings which the disciples experienced involved the senses of sight and sound. No one can deny this since Peter himself said, "This Jesus . . . hath shed forth this (the Holy Spirit), which ye now

see and hear" (Acts 2:32-33). This filling was accompanied
by unusual, sensible manifestations. More about this later
when we study the steps in yielding one's life to the Spirit.

If we agree that the filling of the Spirit refers to the complete control of a Christian by the Spirit, then we may
reasonably inquire –

WHY MUST WE BE FILLED WITH THE SPIRIT?

First, it is needful because God has commanded it. Here
in this verse, and throughout the Bible we are taught that the
wise and happy man is the one who allows God to control
his life in its entirety.

Second, it is imperative because of the nature of man. The
divine estimate of man's heart is this: " . . . the imagination
of man's heart is evil from his youth" (Genesis 8:21). Because
of our tendency toward evil, we need the power of the Holy
Spirit to understand and even desire to practice the laws of
God. Our Lord voiced the same truth when He said, " . . .
without me ye can do nothing" (John 15:5). Man continually
thinks that he amounts to something and has, in himself,
the desire and the will power to follow God. The Galatians
had lapsed back into fleshly efforts to please God. Paul
rebuked them with this question: "Are ye so foolish? having
begun in the Spirit, are ye now made perfect by the flesh"
(Galatians 3:3).

*Third, we need the Spirit's control because of supernatural
responsibilities.* For example, we are told to "give thanks
always for all things" (Ephesians 5:20). In our own strength
we find it difficult to maintain a continual attitude of gratitude – let alone to be thankful for *all things.* Again, who among
us can "bring into captivity every thought to the obedience
of Christ." (II Corinthians 10:5), or "Rejoice in the Lord
alway" (Philippians 4:4)?

Specifically, how can I experience the definite help of the Spirit in my everyday life? How can I realize the complete control or filling of the Spirit?

Before answering that question several points need to be made. First, the Holy Spirit is sovereign. He brings believers to the fulness of Christian living by different avenues or emphases. Dr. V. Raymond Edman's book, *They Found the Secret,* bears abundant evidence to this fact, as does the Bible and church history. Second, the Bible nowhere states and labels the steps we will mention for being filled with the Spirit. To assume any particular approach is false, however, on these grounds and without a personal study of the Scriptures in view of the teaching is naievete or crude dogmatism.

If such steps exist in the Bible, they should be sought, studied, formulated and tested. Such a recipe or formula for a satisfying relationship with the Spirit must meet two tests: (1) it must be the teaching of the Scripture; (2) it must work. The author has tested this viewpoint in his personal life for a period of six years and has found it to meet the test of practice. He believes it is also the teaching of the Bible. The sincere believer, however, is never to stop being a learner. He is a disciple, ever ready to learn from his Teacher.

No teaching involving a personal relationship should be set forth dogmatically in theory, be allowed to bypass the test of everyday reality, and then be used as a cold, lifeless doctrine to which the experiences of all believers must be forced to fit.

As the primary step in coming under the control of the Spirit I must concede that I need His power, and that without God's enablement I can do nothing or be nothing worthwhile in the sight of God. Such an admission comes from an honest appraisal of my capacity to please God and to walk in

His ways. I simply cannot walk with God in my own strength. It was this very characteristic of man's nature, that of being "weak through the flesh," that made the Law ineffective and made necessary the new "law of the Spirit of life in Christ Jesus" (Romans 8:2-4).

The Old Testament prophet Jeremiah voiced the same concept when speaking of man's incapacity to direct his own steps. He said, "O Lord, I know that the way of man is not in himself: it is not in man that walketh to direct his steps" (Jeremiah 10:23). The Apostle Paul seconded this when he wrote, "For I know that in me, (that is, in my flesh,) dwelleth no good thing; for to will is present with me; but how to perform that which is good I find not" (Romans 7:18).

We dare not think that in our own strength we would consistently read the Bible, talk with God, or be concerned about our own spiritual welfare. We do not have the inner capacity to turn ourselves Godward. Any spiritual longings we have come from God. He takes the initiative as the psalmist says, "Blessed is the man whom thou choosest, and causest to approach unto thee, that he may dwell in thy courts" (Psalm 65:4). "We love him, because he first loved us" (I John 4:19). Without the ministry of the Word of God and the Holy Spirit in drawing us to God we would be like the people Paul described to the Philippians, "All the others seem to be wrapped up in their own affairs and do not really care for the business of Jesus Christ" (Philippians 2:21).

THE WEAK SHALL BE MADE STRONG

Our admission of weakness apart from God is the A B C of spiritual living. The believer who believes that he can generate the power and desire to please God or to manage his own life lives in a world of illusion. Given time, and sufficient stress, his world will crumble. Until it does, his spiritual growth will be stunted by a shallow, superficial conformity to accepted spiritual standards and taboos, a holy masquerade, if you will.

In this state he will need to consider, sooner or later, Paul's questioning rebuttal of such a "puffed up" state. He wrote, "For who maketh thee to differ from another? and what hast thou that thou didst not receive? now if thou didst receive it, why dost thou glory (boast) as if thou hadst not received it?" (I Corinthians 4:7). If there are spiritual qualities in our lives, they originated with God.

After assuming the attitude of total dependency upon God for spiritual energy and vitality, another step must be taken.

THE CONFESSION OF KNOWN SIN

This second step is to confess and forsake any known sin present in my life. This is necessary because the Bible teaches throughout that God desires His people to be clean vessels. The responsibility for possessing and maintaining spiritual cleanness is ours, not God's. God commands us in James 4:8, *"Cleanse your hands, ye sinners; and purify your hearts, ye doubleminded."* Both verbs are commands. In II Corinthians 7:1 we read, " ... let us *cleanse ourselves* from all filthiness of the flesh and spirit, perfecting holiness in the fear of God." In the above verses we see that both our *actions* and *attitudes* are to be cleansed and purified. But how can I cleanse myself of sin? By confession. "If we confess our sins, he is faithful and just to forgive us our sins, and *to cleanse us from all unrighteousness"* (I John 1:9).

Our part in the cleansing process is to come to God in confession; then, and not until then, He does the cleansing. Such confession is likely to be accompanied by some emotion. In the book of James we find a description of a sinner cleansing himself in the presence of God.

"Draw nigh to God, and he will draw nigh to you. Cleanse your hands, ye sinners; and purify your hearts, ye double minded. Be afflicted, and mourn, and weep: let your laughter be turned to mourning, and your joy to heaviness. Humble yourselves in the sight of the Lord, and He shall lift you up" (James 4:8-10).

Notice the reversal of emotional patterns. Lightheartedness to seriousness, laughter to mourning, and joy to heaviness. Confession is a serious business. It involves facing the reality of my own basic sinfulness and specific acts of sin. More emotive words would be hard to find. True confession includes contrition or consciousness of guilt and easily leads to a genuinely broken spirit and heart. Compare Psalm 51.

Sincere confession involves the whole person: his mind, his emotions, and his body. It is a real, person-to-person relationship. By faith we draw nigh to God and He draws nigh to us. As this divine-human encounter takes place our attention will be centered on our sins and guilt – and on our God.

It seems to me that some emotional reaction – small or great, hidden or observable – will accompany confession. We will be radically moved by the vileness of our sin and the lovingkindness of our God in forgiving us. This does not mean that confession must always be accompanied by either slight or remarkable emotional stirrings. It may or it may not. In individuals the reaction will be conditioned by the temperament and past experiences of the person involved.

ARE YOU SANGUINE OR PHLEGMATIC?

To illustrate, two Christians attend an evangelistic meeting and observe a friend receive Christ. The excitable, sanguine fellow rushes to his newly converted friend at the first possible moment. Tearfully and with many words and gestures, he congratulates the convert. The other Christian, a calm, phlegmatic person, meets the new convert at the church exit, walks slowly over to him and says, "You made an important decision tonight."

Are both men sincere? Yes, quite likely. But they manifest their gladness in extremely different ways because of their temperament and background. Likewise, believers may react differently to the act of confession. The validity, reality, and sincerity of the confession is not dependent on either the nature of or the extent of the outward reaction. God is concerned with our spirit; not the quantity of our tears.

But what sins, specifically, shall we confess? All we are aware of. A person can not confess sins which he cannot remember. The fact is that at any given time we can only remember, and thus be aware of, "X" number of sins: these should be confessed. Sins which we are not aware of having committed or sins of ignorance are to be dealt with when they come to our attention. This was the practice followed in Old Testament times. See Leviticus 4.

Since we tend to forget unpleasant incidents, we should, after we have confessed all known sin, pray as did the Psalmist, "Search me, O God, and know my heart: try me, and know my thoughts: and see if there be any wicked way in me, and lead me in the way everlasting" (Psalm 139:23-24). If we will quietly wait before the Lord with an open mind, He will direct our attention to sins which need to be confessed.

True confession also involves the intention of honestly forsaking the sin. As the writer of Proverbs points out, "He that covereth his sins shall not prosper: but whoso confesseth *and forsaketh* them shall have mercy" (Proverbs 28:13). If I simply do not desire to give up some sin, I should admit this fact to God, and ask Him to give me the desire and power to forsake it. It has been my experience that God will answer such prayers.

If it is argued that such an approach to confession is too mechanical, apt to become routine, and meaningless, I agree. That is only to say, however, that the parts that make up the whole of any relationship – marital, spiritual, or social – can be performed in a mechanical, unenthusiastic, cut-and-dried, lifeless spirit. It is not the procedure which is at fault, but the spirit of the person or persons involved.

Heartfelt confession includes the fact and experience of *accepting forgiveness;* otherwise it is incomplete. If a person confesses his sin and then still allows feelings of guilt to torment him, his confession is only partial. He is like the man who was carrying a sack of grain up a hill when a man with a horse and wagon offered him a ride. He accepted the ride but rode in the wagon to the top of the hill with *the grain still on his back.* His explanation: he was helping the horse carry the load!

God does not need our help. When, in all sincerity, we confess our sins, we should then by faith consider the matter closed and not allow guilt feelings to ruin our mental health and happiness. When God forgives our sins, he buries them in the depth of the sea; He also, someone has said, erects a sign which says, No FISHING ALLOWED.

After honest and thorough confession you can rise to walk in newness of life, with a sense of cleanness, because God has cleansed you. Then what?

Then you are ready to take the third step toward being controlled or filled with the Spirit: *Surrender your will unconditionally to God.* Your submission will involve relinquishing control of your life to the Spirit. Your lips, mind, hands, time, talent, money, possessions, reputation, and future plans are transferred into His name, signed over to Him. In experience such a yielding may be a once-for-all decision or it may come as a growing conviction that all you are and have are subject to God's control.

Practically, this means that you will continually submit your life to the teachings of the Word of God. You will keep bringing every area of your life into the light of God's Word and will see that it conforms to the will of God.

Once you have taken these steps you are a clean, yielded vessel. This is the will of God for His children and these are

God's conditions for the filling of the Spirit. Now, by faith you can claim the filling of the Spirit. *At this point in time,* as far as you know there is no known sin in your life. You are filled or controlled by the Spirit. You may not feel any different than you did before meeting these conditions, other than the confidence that you are clean before God, and dependent on Him to keep yourself cleansed.

Certain characteristics reveal the man who is Spirit filled. Let's consider these and see if we meet God's requirements . . . .

5

MARKS OF THE SPIRIT-FILLED BELIEVER

What are the signs of being Spirit-filled? In this chapter we will examine false notions about the Spirit's filling a believer, review the meaning of being "filled with the Spirit," and point out the characteristics of a Spirit-filled Christian.

The filling of the Spirit does not mean the believer thus becomes instantaneously mature at some mystical, dramatic moment. In all the kingdoms of this world – animal, vegetable, mineral, or spiritual – growth and maturity constitute a gradual process, not an instant act. The animal is conceived, born, lives and dies; each phase takes its own time and is preceded by a process made up of separate acts. A tree grows from seed to sapling to maturity – its life is a process. The diamond is produced gradually by the enormous heat and pressure of sand and mud. It takes years for the carbon to crystallize into the almost complete purity of a diamond.

To expect instantaneous maturity in the spiritual realm, then, is to deny the laws of growth. We grow mentally, morally, emotionally, and spiritually – there may be periods of rapid growth in one or more of these areas, but God offers no miracle tonic producing on-the-spot maturity.

Another false notion about the Spirit-filled life is the dangerous suggestion of a once-for-all victory over sin; that if we are filled with the Spirit of God we will never again suffer spiritual defeat. This idea is doubly dangerous. First, it is not true to the Bible or the experience of saints. Second, it raises false hopes which will surely crumble under the pressures of everyday life. When this happens, the misled believer loses confidence in God because his faith was in a lie.

Day after day every believer is bombarded by numerous kinds of temptation, small and hidden, as well as large and obvious. It will be so until he dies, although the temptations will change and, it is hoped, he will develop stronger spiritual muscles. To suggest, however, that some experience, no matter how thrilling or unusual, will make him immune to temptation's pull or give him adequate spiritual stamina to withstand all temptation is misleading and false.

The same marks characterize any teaching of sinless perfection, a wholly sanctified life, or claims to absolute holiness. Such assertions are misleading and out of touch with true spiritual reality if they exclude the possibility of sin.

Then what does it mean to "be filled with the Spirit"?

It means to be controlled by the Holy Spirit.

This can be seen by examining the text itself. It says, "Be not drunk with wine wherein is excess." What characterizes a drunk man? He is controlled by the wine, the spirits within him. He has, in varying degrees, lost his self-control to spirit-control.

To be filled with the Spirit involves losing self-control to Spirit-control. In this case, however, the mind and will is sharpened and strengthened – not dulled and weakened.

Notice that a drunk man's fulness of spirit can be measured quantitatively. Some states use such tests to determine if a driver suspected of drunk driving is legally drunk. Degrees of spirit-control show up in the worldly man's description of his partner's drunkenness, namely, "He's just a little tight." "He's two sheets in the wind." "He's stone drunk; he can't even move!"

Likewise the fulness of the Spirit varies in degree. It is said of Jesus that he had the Spirit without measure (John 3:34). Of no other man can that be said. Thus, the filling of the Spirit does not mean in the case of men, absolute 100 percent, every-second, in-all-areas, control. This quality of fulness of the Spirit belonged to Jesus only. It was the Apostle's prayer that Christians might "be filled with all the fulness of God" (Ephesians 3:19b).

With this qualified definition of being filled with the Spirit in mind, what then are the marks of the Spirit-filled life?

(1) *The Spirit-filled Christian has no known sin in his life.* This is not to say he is without sin. *But* it does mean that he is not aware of any specific sin. When a specific sin is brought to his attention by the Spirit, the regular reading of the Word, his wife, or any means, he will be more likely to confess it than will his Christian brother who is allowing sin to weaken his power to hear God's voice and to obey God's commands. This is true because –

(2) *The Spirit-filled Christian has yielded his life to God.* He has crossed the Rubicon and has burned his bridges. Having voluntarily enlisted with God for active service, he refuses, by the Spirit's power, to seriously consider seeking a discharge.

Needless to say, time and again he is tempted to quit, to betray his initial decision. But, as God strengthens him, he is kept from turning back. Each day, in fact each minute, he will face the consequences of his initial decision. To will "once for all" to have God as one's master is followed by the not unpleasant moment-by-moment enticements to have one's own way. Thus, to yield once to God leads necessarily to yielding again and again and again day after day until we are with Him.

Because of this process of maturity –

(3) *The Spirit-filled Christian is gradually and increasingly controlled by the Spirit.* As the Apostle put it in Philippians 3:13, "Yet, my brothers, I do not consider myself already perfect. But I keep going on . . . ." The Christian never arrives – he is always going on toward maturity.

Gradually, as the Spirit convicts and empowers him he sheds habits and attitudes that displease God and "puts on the new man" (Ephesians 4:24).

Increasingly, the Spirit-filled Christian yields new areas of his life to the Spirit's control. In short, he grows spiritually. Yes, there will be periods of quiescence, of dormancy when he seems to stand still. This, too, is part of the process of growth into maturity. Moreover, he will fall short, he will fail, he will sin. But the truly regenerate will rise again. "For a just man falleth seven times, and riseth up again" (Proverbs 24:16). The Spirit-filled Christian echoes the words of John the Baptist, "He must increase, but I must decrease" (John 3:30). Such a Christian is in the process of "increasing in the knowledge of God" (Colossians 1:10c).

(4) *The Spirit-filled Christian is radically controlled by the Holy Spirit.* This means he is radically extreme, thorough-going, and even drastic in his obedience to, and love for, God.

He progressively seeks with God's help to fulfil the first and greatest commandment, "Thou shalt love the Lord thy God with *all thy heart* and with *all thy soul,* and with *all thy mind*" (Matthew 22:37).

As he seeks actively to let God, who is Love, control the depth of his being, he also desires that God's will be done in each of his varied roles. He wishes to be a Spirit-filled husband, father, employee, Sunday school teacher, or whatever.

Thus the Spirit-filled Christian does not easily fall into the trap psychologists call *compartmental thinking*, i.e. the tendency to separate one's roles in such a way as to prohibit interrelationships. We've all heard of businessmen who profess Christianity but do not apply it to their business transactions. Surely the Spirit-filled Christian will have blind spots, or areas where he grows slowly, but he is less likely to than the Christian who does not walk moment by moment in the Spirit, as Christians are commanded to do. He is less likely to be hypocritical because the changes in his life, at his conversion and following it, did not stop at the surface of his personality, they reached down to the very root.

(5) *The Spirit-filled Christian is continually controlled by the Holy Spirit.* By continual we do not mean unceasing or perpetual. Rather, we mean a control which, though not unbroken, is certainly renewed after each interruption. Thus the literal translation of the central passage on the filling of the Spirit is "be being kept filled with the Spirit." Whereas the unyielded Christian allows "minor" sins to pile up, so to speak, the Spirit's control of the spiritual Christian helps him to confess and forsake his sin quickly, and prevents a prolonged break in communion.

(6) *The Spirit-filled Christian is confidently, consciously and sensitively controlled by the Holy Spirit. Confidence* means "a mental attitude of relying on a worthy person, a state of trust or intimacy between persons who confide in each other." As the Christian walks with the Spirit each day, seeking His advice and strength, he learns to rely on the Holy Spirit and to confide in Him moment by moment. It is this type of control that marks the life of the Spirit-filled Christian.

The *conscious* control of the believer by the Spirit is often misunderstood. Again and again believers are warned not to trust their emotions, to suspect their religious feelings. Granted, one can be misled by his emotions. But that is no reason to assume a suspicious attitude toward all emotions. To do so can easily lead to a dull, humdrum, phlegmatic, emotionally detached Christian life. One does not love another with all his heart, soul, and mind without some emotional involvement!

Remember that God is a person and He has chosen to become emotionally involved with His creatures. The Father *so loved that He gave* His Son, and the Holy Spirit can be grieved or hurt by our sin. It is said in the Bible that Christians are married to Christ (Romans 7:4), can you conceive of a more intimately emotional relationship?

Now to be *conscious* of something means "to see, hear, feel, or allow to enter one's mind." It involves an awareness of one's surroundings and the numerous nearby stimuli.

If you took a walk with a friend you would surely be conscious of his or her presence. Christians are told to "walk in (and by) the Spirit" (Galatians 5:16, 25), and one name of the Spirit, the Comforter, means "one called alongside to help." God, the Holy Spirit, dwells within us and is therefore ever with us. The question is, can we be conscious or aware of His presence?

I believe we can and indeed we must if we ever hope to walk with God, obey His voice, and know Him personally. Someone may say, "But we walk by faith, not feeling." I disagree. We do not depend on feelings but they are a vital and valid part of our Christian walk. I believe that faith in the *living* God leads to a conscious experience of His presence through our awakened senses.

For example, we are told "He that hath an ear, let him hear what the Spirit saith unto the churches" (Revelation 3:6). This clearly speaks of a conscious experience. Also we are told "We are of God: he that knoweth God heareth us; he that is not of God heareth not us" (II John 4:6).

The Spirit "teaches" believers and helps them remember the words of Jesus (John 14:26), He testifies to the believer in Christ (John 15:26), He guides the believer into all truth, speaks what he hears, and shows us the things of Christ (John 16:14).

If the Spirit does all this, it should be obvious He is not a mute teacher. He speaks and we hear. It may be a still small voice, a clear word of rebuke, a verse brought to mind, a passage read in daily devotions, a sermon or a strong and clear impression that we should or should not do a certain thing. (To avoid being led astray such messages should be tested by the clear teaching of the Word of God; if any impression or leading violates or contradicts the Bible it is not the voice of the Holy Spirit.)

With this qualification one thing remains clear, such hearing of the voice of the Spirit must be realized to be understood and obeyed; it need not be audible, and seldom is, but it must be understandable. As the Apostle wrote in a similar context, "For if the trumpet give an uncertain sound, who shall prepare himself to the battle?" (I Corinthians 14:8). Our Commanding Officer does not mumble His orders. He speaks loud enough for alert soldiers to get the message.

Thus we may say that the Spirit-filled Christian is *sensitively* controlled by the Holy Spirit. As he hears and obeys the Spirit's voice, he develops a spiritual awareness. To use two of the apostle's phrases, he "walks circumspectly" (Ephesians 5:15) or he is "led by the Spirit of God" (Romans 8:14). As he refuses to allow any known sin to remain unconfessed, as he continues walking daily by faith and yielding his attitudes, habits, dispositions, words, and thoughts to the Spirit's control, he will experience the conscious presence of the Holy Spirit, he will be practicing the presence of God.

To enumerate the marks of a Spirit-filled life, however, is both useless and dangerous unless we are voluntarily and actively involved daily in the process of "walking in the Spirit." If we fail to "exercise ourselves unto godliness" by making daily use of all the means of grace at our disposal, the real and intimate presence of God will not be a reality in our own experience.

May we all pray with the Apostle that we "might be filled with all the fulness of God" (Ephesians 3:19) and that "the God of hope will fill us with all joy and peace in believing, that we may abound in hope, through the power of the Holy Ghost" (Romans 15:13).

Are you filled with the Spirit? If not, why not?

The privilege is yours. Christ died, rose again, and ascended into heaven that the Holy Spirit could invade and control your life. Why not let Him right now? The next chapter tells you how to make your friendship with the Holy Spirit an everyday experience, how to fulfill the apostle's command to "walk in the Spirit."

6

HOW TO WALK IN THE SPIRIT DAY BY DAY

The Bible commands us to walk in (or by) the Spirit. Walking in the Spirit is the result of being controlled or filled with the Spirit. The Bible also promises that if we walk in the Spirit we will not fulfil the lust of the flesh (Galatians 5:16). Since all sin enters a Christian's life after he is "drawn away of his own lust and enticed" it follows that this is a promise of victory over sin.

The question remains: *What does it mean to "walk in the Spirit"?* The word walk is used two ways in the New Testament, literally ("the lame walk"), and figuratively ("walk in the light"). The first refers to the physical act of moving; the latter to the process of living or the actions and attitudes that make up our day-to-day walk. Thus, the word "walk" refers to one's inner and outer behavior, the entire scope of one's life.

The second question is: *What does "in (or by) the Spirit" mean?* The case of the noun "Spirit" in this verse is instrumental: We are to walk by means of the Spirit. It also includes the notion of association or accompaniment.[1] Thus, the verse might be paraphrased as, "Live your whole life by the power of, and in the presence of, the Spirit."

With this background in mind let us attempt to answer the question, *"How can we walk in the Spirit?"* At least three questions need to be answered: (1) "How can I bring my everyday life under the power of the Spirit?" (2) "How can I associate or fellowship with the Spirit?" and (3) "How can I experience the presence of the Spirit in my everyday life?"

In chapters four and five we considered the marks of the Spirit-filled Christian and how to be filled with the Spirit. This answers *how* we can *begin* the life of fellowship with the Spirit. *Continued communion* or a walk with the Holy Spirit involves two broad areas: our roles in the life and the Bible; and two basic principles: freedom from known sin and obedience to the Spirit's leading.

WALKING IN THE SPIRIT: POSITIVE AND NEGATIVE ASPECTS

Since our lives consist of numerous roles, living our whole life in the Spirit involves a positive, conscious effort on our part to build our roles in life on the values revealed by the Holy Spirit in the Bible. Negatively, it calls also for the elimination of habits and attitudes not pleasing to God.

WALKING IN THE SPIRIT: OUR RESPONSIBILITY

But you ask, is not the conscious effort to build stronger Christian character in our lives an evidence of fleshly effort? *No!* The fact is we are exhorted in numerous places to be actively involved in the process of sanctification. Here are a few sample passages:

[1]Robertson and Davis, *A New Short Grammar of the Greek Testament,* Harper and Brothers Publishers, New York, 1933, p. 239.

And beside this, *giving all diligence, add* to your faith virtue; and to virtue knowledge; And to knowledge temperance; and to temperance patience; and to patience godliness; And to godliness brotherly kindness; and to brotherly kindness charity (II Peter 1:5-7).

But whoso looketh into the perfect law of liberty, and *continueth therein,* he being not a forgetful hearer, but a doer of the work, this man shall be blessed in his deed (James 1:25).

But refuse profane and old wives' fables, and *exercise* thyself rather unto godliness. *Meditate* upon these things; *give thyself* wholly to them; that thy profiting may appear to all. *Take heed* unto thyself, and unto the doctrine; *continue* in them: for in doing this thou shalt both save thyself, and them that hear thee (I Timothy 4:7, 15, 16).

But ye, beloved, *building up yourselves* on your most holy faith, praying in the Holy Ghost (Jude 20).

But he answered and said, It is written, Man shall not live by bread alone, *but by every word* that proceedeth out of the mouth of God (Matthew 4:4). But his delight is in the law of the Lord; and in his law doth he *meditate day and night* (Psalm 1:2).

Study (or give diligence) to shew thyself approved unto God, a workman that needeth not to be ashamed, rightly dividing the word of truth (II Timothy 2:15).

One distinguishing factor between fleshly effort and sanctified effort is the motive. If I "exercise myself unto godliness" out of a spirit of dread or as an attempt to make myself acceptable to God, then I frustrate the grace of God because righteousness does not come by keeping rules – it is a gift from God (Galatians 2:21).

But, walking by the Spirit means a regular, active and *diligent* use of all the means of grace with the strength imparted by the Spirit. Prayer, meditation on the words of God, church attendance, fellowship with other Christians, the use of one's time, personal evangelism, giving, in fact, all of the graces serve to help us bring our lives under the control of God's Spirit.

Thus to walk in the Spirit involves the total process of sanctification as every role of one's life is conformed to the Spirit's will – the Word of God.

IN CASE OF SIN . . .

We suggested earlier that walking in the Spirit includes two basic principles, *freedom from known sin* and *obedience to the Spirit's leading.* When the believer who is walking in the Spirit's power lapses into walking in his own strength, he has succumbed to temptation and sin. Then he must follow the Spirit's directions for cleansing as found in I John 1:9. By confessing and forsaking his sin he returns to relying on the Spirit's power in his walk.

In daily Bible study as well as in contacts with people the Holy Spirit's purpose is to provide not only doctrine, but reproof, corrections, instruction in righteousness "that the man of God may be perfect, thoroughly furnished unto all good works" (II Timothy 3:16).

In our daily reading of the Word, the Holy Spirit reveals specific sins and leads us to confess and forsake them. If we resist His ministry we grieve and quench the Holy Spirit (cf. Ephesians 4:30 and I Thessalonians 5:21). When this happens, the Spirit no longer controls us, and we are walking in our own strength and in known sin. In such a case we are out of fellowship with the Spirit and may, if we insist on our own way, experience the loving chastening of our Father. If we continue to disobey God's commandments we may lose our assurance of salvation (Compare John 14:21,23; I John 2:3-5 and I John 4:18-21) and since we are sowing to the flesh, we will manifest in some degree the works of the flesh (Galatians 6:7,8 and 5:19-21).

On the other hand as we walk in the Spirit He will produce in us His fruits: love, joy, peace, longsuffering, gentleness, goodness, faith, meekness, and temperance (self-control) (Galatians 5: 22, 23). (See the next chapter.)

Some might feel that "walking in the Spirit" is an attitude and that we do an injustice to suggest it be "lowered" to the level of everyday life and behavior. A preoccupation with mystical experiences, however, unrelated to daily life leads to an unreal spirituality that is foreign to the Word of God.

The person who speaks of having "no known sin" in his life *but* who neglects the means of grace such as prayer and the regular reading of the Word is, by his neglect, living in known sin. This is a perversion of the truth and produces, at best, a false, insecure, peace.

Since living in the Word is such a vital part of our spiritual walk, a later chapter will offer definite guidelines to help Christians make daily Bible reading a sacred habit and an exciting adventure.

Now let's consider several guidelines to a positive walk in the Spirit as it relates to the reading of the Word and the building of a Biblically sound value system.

Everyday life in the Spirit involves daily, meaningful Bible reading. *The Christian who is walking in the Spirit obeys the exhortation of the Bible to take time daily to meditate on the Word of God.* This gives him strength and sustenance for the day. It helps him discover sins of attitude or action in his life and confess them. It can also be a time of consciously building his own value system based on the Word of God. I have found it edifying to read through the New Testament seeking to find the teaching of the Bible on my role as a father, employee, etc.

Aside from the father-role, typical married male roles include husband, sweetheart, provider, neighbor, employee, citizen, and churchworker. Major married female roles include wife, lover, mother, housekeeper, homemaker, neighbor, citizen, and churchworker.

A role could be defined as a set of behaviors which is typical of the occupants of a particular position. A role is in no sense an actor's role. It is a composite of habits typical of a given position, such as those above.

Nothing can take the place of the Spirit-controlled Christian studying his own Bible with a view to understanding his own roles, and being "fully persuaded in his own mind" as to his personal responsibilities. As an example a woman could set apart a month in her personal devotions to study her role as a wife. Such a procedure gives meaning and direction to one's Bible reading. The same plan can be followed by an unmarried Christian as he studies his roles as boyfriend, employee, personal worker, etc.

In making one's own study and conclusions on his various roles (this could easily involve years of personal study of one's roles as set forth in the Bible), one could also read what has been written by Christian leaders *and secular writers.* Two articles setting forth the views of a leading Christian psychologist are: "Keep Your Roles in Balance," a *Moody Monthly* Reprint and "Understanding Your Roles" chapter 4 of the Scripture Press book, *Building A Christian Home* both by Dr. Henry Brandt and Homer Dowdy.

After testing your own Bible study conclusions by Christian experts in the field of human behavior, you would profit by understanding the secular viewpoint and adapting it to *your Christian* Biblical view.

Two books on this subject for women are Morton Hunt's *Her Infinite Variety* and Betty Friedan's *The Femine Mystique.* In reading these books the Christian bears in mind that *his* value system is determined by, and founded on, the principles revealed in the Bible. Where no Biblical principle can be discovered he seeks God's will by prayer, reading, enlightened reasoning, and consultation with others.

As the Spirit-controlled Christian examines his roles in the light of the Word he will discover weak areas in his role-fulfilment. In practice this could mean that he senses a laxness in his role performance, say as a father. To remedy this he meditates on what the Bible teaches about the principles of Christian fatherhood. Then he prayerfully seeks God's power to help him conform his father-role to the Word.

As a further aid to bringing my entire life under the Spirit's control I've found it helpful to list a different role on my prayer list for each day of the week. This means that as I meditate on the Word of God and also consider my own performance I prayerfully seek the Spirit's help in conforming my conduct to the teaching of the Word of God.

At this point some readers may be saying, "This fellow is making a walk with the Spirit a matter of work, study, discipline and diligence. I thought walking in another's power and presence would be easy, exciting and glamorous."

And so it is. But walking involves effort; discipleship includes discipline and study and diligence. Jesus said, "If ye *continue in my word,* then are ye my disciples indeed; and ye shall know the truth, and the truth shall make you free."

The Jews claimed they had never been in bondage to any man and then asked, "How sayest thou, 'Ye shall be made free'?"

Jesus' answer was, "Verily, verily, I say unto you, Whosoever committeth sin is the servant (slave) of sin . . . If the Son therefore shall make you free, ye shall be free indeed" (John 8:31-36).

The Christian who does not continue in His Word and refuses to shape his life by its teaching becomes a *slave* to himself, to sin, and to a purely secular value system. The believer who joins his will with the power of the Spirit and continues to mold his life by Jesus' words day by day becomes "free indeed." Why? Because freedom only comes by continual surrender to the Spirit's will – the Word of God.

But many disciples have tried to "let the Word of Christ dwell in them richly," to allow Christ's words to abide in them, and to "meditate day and night in the Word," only to fail. After many attempts to maintain a practice of daily Bible reading, hundreds of believers have given up, discouraged and guilt-laden.

The next chapter is designed to offer help. The author failed consistently for ten years – then God undertook. He will help you too.

7

HOW TO ENJOY THE BIBLE

There is no such thing as victory over sin and a joyful walk with the Spirit unless we turn repeatedly, frequently, and meaningfully to the sacred, Spirit-breathed pages of the Holy Scriptures.

If you find Bible study and reading an irksome duty rather than a delightful habit, let me suggest several approaches which will increase the value and quality of your daily trysts with the Lord.

1. *To hear the voice of the Spirit, your Teacher, your life must be free from any known sin.* Freedom from *known* sin opens your ears to hear what the Spirit says through the Word. If I am *consciously* harboring resentment, secretly fondling a pet sin, or admittedly neglecting a spiritual responsibility my hearing will be dulled, my spiritual vision will be blurred, and my appetite for the Word of God will ebb. To walk in known sin is to grieve the Holy Spirit and we are told "Grieve not the Holy Spirit" (Ephesians 4:30). We have a responsibility to *"cleanse ourselves* from all

filthiness of the flesh *and spirit,* perfecting holiness in the
fear of God" (II Corinthians 7:1).

We must judge and cleanse ourselves (I Corinthians 11:31)
by confessing and forsaking all known sin (I John 1:9 and
Proverbs 28:13). This sort of confession is no routine matter.
It must be an affair of the heart.

2. *To profit spiritually from the reading of God's Word
your will must be willed to obey God.* You can, and should,
determine by a definite choice to obey God's message to you
from His Word – without any reservations. When we disobey
God's clear message to us we quench or stifle the Spirit
and we are warned, "Quench not the Spirit" (I Thessalonians 5:19). We can choose to obey whatever God commands.
To do less is to pretend. If you do not intend to obey God's
Word at the moment He speaks to you, then why bother
to read? Why bother to pray? Why bother to listen to the
pastor? In fact, why bother to *play act* the Christian life
if it is not worth *being?*

Does It Take Time to Be Holy?

3. *To receive a definite message from God through His
Word you must take time.* You will never *find* time; there
are always "more important" things to do. The only way
to find time is to make it. You must tell yourself, "I will
take time to read God's Word every day." And then *do*
it. Allow *nothing* to interfere. Your relationships with your
husband, your children, your church, your house, your job
and your community *must* not interfere with your walk with
God. God and His Word come first; then as a result of a
healthy, vibrant walk with and by the Spirit every role of
your life will become God-saturated. This is the joyful adventure and daily process of "being filled (controlled) with-
and-by the Spirit" (Ephesians 5:18).

But unless we take time alone with God and His Word

and let His Spirit teach us, we rob ourselves out of the thrill of walking intimately with our Father. The sad truth is that we always find time for the things we need. Are we genuinely convinced that we *need* to spend more time alone with God over His Word?

4. *To receive a message from God through His Word you must take enough time.*

No certain amount of time is sacred. But you must allow *enough* time so you can read leisurely without having to worry about retiring at a reasonable hour, getting off to work on time, or keeping the kids out of your hair.

If you begin by providing something like a half hour or more to spend daily in prayer and Bible reading – and if you keep at it day after day in a prayerful, expectant attitude, the Holy Spirit will meet with you in a real way.

This does not mean that you will be confined hereafter to an hour or less of spiritual exercise. You may well find that your time of reading and prayer will extend over the alloted time. Or, it may take less time to hear God speak to you. Hearing His voice daily is not measured by, or dependent on, how much time you spend. It should involve genuine communication between you and the Holy Spirit. Such communication is the result of the illuminating ministry of the Holy Spirit through the Word of God.

My own experience has been that when I finally was willing and enabled to give God at least an hour a day, He would often speak to me in the first few minutes of reading. When this happened I would stop reading and meditate on the meaning of this message for my life. I would pray it into my mind and *anticipate* how I might live it out in my life that day. How, I would ask the Lord, should this truth influence my thoughts, words, and actions today? And then I would pause and listen to what the Spirit would teach me as a member of His Church (Revelation 3:22).

The prevalent habit of finishing the chapter or book and

then reconsidering what God has said to us may prove harmful. We may forget that particular verse or phrase that communicated to us *as we read it.* When the Spirit speaks we must be willing to stop, look, and listen.

We are not built to receive and assimilate multiplied blessings, warnings, or rebukes at one sitting. To retain one lesson in our thoughts, to translate it into our actions, and to pass it on to our brethren constitutes part of the challenge of practicing the presence of God moment by moment, of walking in the Spirit.

If you have allowed plenty of time, you can spend the remainder of it in prayer, in memorizing the striking passage, or other forms of spiritual exercise.

DISCIPLINE AND DELIGHT: WHICH COMES FIRST?

5. *To take time each day with the Lord and His Word, you will have to discipline yourself daily.* Actually this Spirit-empowered self-control is an important by-product of a quiet hour. Any time you *will to do* anything of a truly spiritual nature you can be sure that your own selfish impulses will throw up roadblocks.

Common messages from the threatened throneroom of the senses are "Oh, I'm so tired this morning, I think I'd be better off to sleep in. I'll read the Bible later." Or, "I know myself too well. I just couldn't get up an hour earlier to read the Bible, so why try?" Or perhaps, "Well, I'm too tired tonight. I'll read *two* chapters tomorrow evening."

Whether you take your time in the morning or in the evening or during the day, other chores will plead and reason with you, "I am more important, I come first," they will insist. To meet such pleas we *must simply determine once for all that communication with God through His Word will have top priority in the daily schedule.*

Such seemingly innocent activities as late-into-the-night

conversations, "important" committee meetings, and late TV programs must undergo an agonizing reappraisal. The "Go-Go-Go" of an organization centered society must be replaced by a firm decision to "Wait (daily) on the Lord." Many Christians have, in the name of Christian service, spread themselves so thin that they have become shallow.

If you make self-discipline in these vital areas a matter of prayer and trust, God will provide the self-control by His Spirit. You, however, must be ruthless in disciplining yourself. Remember a hurried, harried on-the-run schedule is probably not a *walk* with and by the Holy Spirit. The responsibility of ordering your steps in His Word (Psalm 119:133) lies at the door of your will.

No one will urge you to stop serving on numerous committees or to refrain from attending church and social functions so you can spend time over the Word and in prayer, strengthening your personal devotional life. Many Christians, judging by their actions, think church service is more important than the daily reading of the Word. They scurry frantically *around* the visible altar while neglecting the invisible altar in their own heart. We must keep in mind that private sanctification prepares us for fruitful public service.

Habits, holy and otherwise, are strengthened by every repetition and weakened by every omission. When several days go by of watching TV half of the night or sleeping in till the last possible moment, your resolution will crumble like shattered pottery. Smashed by your own hand with the hammer of self-gratification.

6. *To profit spiritually from your Bible reading, avoid competing with a Read-the-Bible-through chart.* If you follow the suggestions outlined above, you will find it impossible to finish a given number of prescribed chapters each day and still assimilate the message of God for your heart. After several days in one chapter you may still be feasting on the first six or eight verses!

Reading the Bible through *is* a commendable practice; but, fellowshiping with the Author as He patiently instructs you in the meaning of His Book is more uplifting and edifying for the inner man. It is my observation that many people have set themselves to read through the Bible in a year only to find their reading lifeless and uninspiring.

ARE YOU BORED WITH THE BIBLE?

7. *To overcome a lack of expectation and a sense of boredom, read in a fresh translation.* These two negative attitudes are invisible Goliaths challenging you from the hilltop to dare enjoy the Bible. Several spiritual maneuvers will help you meet this challenge. One is to pray fervently and faithfully for an expectant attitude and anointed eyes as the psalmist did. "Open thou mine eyes, that I may behold wondrous things out of thy law" (Psalm 119:18).

Keep your motive clearly in mind. You are not reading the Bible because a Christian ought to read it, or because the pastor urges you to. You read God's Word because you *need* food for the inner man (Matthew 4:4) and because you are consciously seeking to know and perform your roles as God instructs you in His Word. You and I have needs which we are not even aware of—only God can minister to such needs. You may need an encouraging word from God to lift a burden, a gentle warning today to keep you from a wrong tomorrow, or a stern reminder from God that your tongue needs to be tied.

A good tactic to beat boredom is to read a fresh, unfamiliar translation of the Scriptures. Consider reading the Phillips Translation, William's Translation, the Berkeley Version, the Amplified Bible, or *Living Letters*. As you read the translation, compare verses with your own study Bible. This practice will bring many thrilling discoveries and open the eyes of your inner man to the richness of the Holy Scriptures.

To avoid losing the value of your reading, copy striking differences in the margin of your Bible.

8. *To fill your mind with God's thoughts, meditate on individual words, phrases and sentences.* Care must always be taken to interpret every passage in keeping with the grammatical, cultural, and historical context. Devotional reading must never sink to sentimentalism, nor should it disregard the laws of grammar. It must combine simple unaffected reverence with humble, enlightened rationalism.

In devotional reading one should watch for and search out the meaning of individual words, descriptive titles of God, and other pregnant phrases.

For example, the psalmist cries in Psalm 90:1, "Lord, Thou hast been our dwelling place in all generations." God Himself was the Abode of the Israelites. And He is our abode too (John 15:5,7). Just think, God is your Dwelling Place! What a place to dwell! Meditate on this great experiential truth, and let it grip your whole being.

WHEN YOU JUST DON'T CARE

9. *To dethrone those temporary depressing moods which many people experience, rest your soul on the breast of God, trusting fully in His mercy and tenderness.* At different times in your walk with the Lord you will probably become discouraged and depressed, for no apparent reason. (Psychiatrists are not always able to trace the source of mood swings and periods of mild depression.) In such a state you just don't care about anything. You are clearly not interested in any form of spiritual exercise. You don't feel like reading, praying, or even thinking about God. What should you do?

One thing must be grasped firmly during such periods – God loves you – and He will continue to love you in spite of your present, temporary depression. Another factor must be kept in mind: God is your best Friend and friends do not desert us at our time of greatest need. As Solomon wrote, "A friend loveth at all times, and a brother is born for adversity" (Proverbs 17:17). Too often we feel that God is peeved at our failures and weaknesses. We forget that He is the "God of patience" (Romans 15:5).

It is probably best to honestly and fully tell the Lord exactly how you feel. Admit your sluggishness, heaviness, and emptiness. Then ask Him for help. "O God, I have little desire to seek You – in fact I have next to none. I know I need to hear Your voice today. I cast myself on Your mercy. Turn my will and my senses to You." It has been my experience that when I was willing to express my depressed feelings to the Lord and to wait before Him, He quickened me or made me alive by His Spirit.

Apparently the psalmist often needed this spiritual reviving. He prayed, for instance, in Psalm 119:28, "My soul melteth for heaviness: strengthen Thou me according unto Thy Word." In verse 35 we read, *"Make me to go* in the path of Thy commandments. . . ." And in the next verse he pleads, *"Incline my heart* unto Thy testimonies, and not to covetousness."

We live in a spiritually barren world that is "no friend of grace to help us on to God." We have, within us and outside of us, forces which can continually dampen our enthusiasm and quench our hunger for God and His Word. But if we will allow ample time for meeting the Lover of our souls, and if we will decide to make this tryst a holy habit of our everyday life, we will, in His time, be able to echo the psalmist's joyful affirmation, "Thy testimonies have I taken as an heritage for ever: for they are *the rejoicing of my heart"* (Psalm 119:111).

As we seek the Holy Spirit's help to enable us to "Walk in the Spirit," as we continue to yield our inner attitudes and outward actions to His control, and as we regularly submit our own roles in life to the standards of the Word of God, we will fulfil the words of the Apostle in our everyday lives;

> Don't let the world around you squeeze you into its own mold, but let God remold your minds from within, so that you may prove in practice that the plan of God for you is good, meets all his demands and moves toward the goal of true maturity (Romans 12:2, Phillips translation).

But this remolding is a process. As such it involves not only the reading of the Word and its application to our daily lives but also the habit of talking everything over with God. We need to know how to enjoy talking with God, how to have "sweet hours of prayer" regularly.

8

IS GOD A STRANGER TO YOU?

When was the last time you spent an hour alone with God? If a friend asked you to join him in an hour of prayer or Bible reading what would be your first reaction? Do you mean it when you sing "Sweet Hour of Prayer"?

The results of a questionnaire given to 75 evangelical Christians indicated that these believers spent about 13 *minutes* a day in prayer. This hardly indicates a consuming love for our privilege of seeking His face in communion.

The sad truth is that God is a stranger to far too many Bible-believing Christians. If ever forced to spend an hour alone with God, many believers would hardly know how to begin, let alone how to commune for a full hour. The fact is we are not really acquainted with God. If God was a close friend we would spend much time with Him – and enjoy it. What is more enjoyable than an evening spent in conversation with an old friend? But when did you last spend an evening with your heavenly Friend?

With a few minutes a day we try to join in on the process and purpose of God to conform us to the image of Christ, to teach us to walk in the Spirit and in unfeigned love.

With a few minutes a day for God we try to build Christian homes, establish new Christian organizations, and increase attendance at God's house. This approach is one of the main reasons that believers fall so short of their spiritual potentialities.

Moreover, it is an insult to Almighty God to give Him only a few minutes a day. Dare I give less time to the feeding of my inner man than I spend satisfying the appetite of the outer man?

Each day provides 1,440 minutes to use or misuse. Everyone receives this allotment. You and I are guilty of abusing time if we fail to meet our Saviour day by day in a warm and meaningful sharing of blessings, thanksgivings, praises, trials, confessions, and anxieties.

Suppose that your spouse came to you after your honeymoon and announced, "Now, darling, I want you to fully understand that I love you with all my heart, my mind, my soul, and my spirit. My love for you will never change no matter what may enter into our lives.

"You know, however, that we live in a world which demands a fast pace; that my job comes first if you expect me to win that promotion – and raise.

"Because of this, it will be essential to our marriage and our economic and social welfare that I spend most of my time in other activities rather than spending a lot of time at home with you. Of course, as it is economically feasible I will try to find a few minutes each day to devote entirely to you."

You laugh! But many Christians are guilty of giving only a few minutes for God, but hours for success, hours for promotion, hours for money, and hours for amusement.

We need to keep in mind that men do not stumble over mountains – they climb mountains, but stumble over mole-hills. The daily quiet *hour* has caused many a saint to stumble. How, they ask, can reading and praying every day be as dreadfully important as many spiritual leaders make out? Is not the prayer closet out of style in our day? Isn't it enough to spend the day in an attitude of prayer?

The Bible? "Oh, I took a course in doctrine so I'm well-grounded in the Bible. Besides, I hear it preached three times a week, isn't that enough?"

No! It won't be, that is, if God is a good Friend of yours. And if you enjoy His presence.

It seems true that many believers do not enjoy their faith in Christ and their walk with Him. Oh, they have peace with God all right; but peace is a passive state. The joy of Christ is a positive emotion lying somewhere between glad-ness and rapture. It doesn't necessarily show itself in a smil-ing face, but it does produce a smiling, rejoicing inner man.

When we first became Christians we happily donned the robes of evangelical conformity. We stopped doing what our group labeled sin and we settled back on the uneasy couch of spiritual conformity, assuring ourselves that we had pleased God.

As innocent babes in Christ we felt compelled to adopt a system of values, a set of ready-made dos and don'ts. For babies, such acceptance of values is excusable and perhaps necessary. The tragedy is that many of us have yet to de-velop our own personal value system based on an independent, Holy Spirit-led study of the Word of God.

This getting-acquainted-with-God-by-hearsay leads us to false notions of what God is like. It will result in a bor-rowed, pseudo-spirituality which can only lead to a shallow and joyless walk with the Lord.

If we hope to get acquainted with God we must spend time poring over the pages of His Autobiography. Spiritual vitality and an intimate knowledge of God must be found in the quiet, unpretentious, and often unrecognized hours spent with the Lord and His Word.

Such daily spiritual trysts will saturate us with the presence of God and help us relate our faith to every area of our daily lives. Short of this – we will face the possibility of spiritual bankruptcy and languishing Christian living.

The choice is ours!

The next chapter offers some guidelines to real, vital prayer.

9

HOW TO ENJOY TALKING WITH GOD

Have you ever experienced "the pure delight of a single hour" spent before the throne of God? Or do you find it impossible to find an hour for prayer?

It seems to me that Christians ought to love to get alone with the Word of God and pray it into their lives. It should be normal for Christians to have long seasons of prayer daily because they love God and enjoy talking with Him. Aside from the joy of His felt presence, we need to bring our weakness to Him that we might be made strong; our sadness to Him that we might be made glad; and our inner conflicts to Him that we might be made peaceful. If our minds are to be "stayed on Him" then we shall have to *stay with Him* in the closet of prayer.

As we spend time with God in prayer and meditation, we will come to love Him and desire His presence every minute. As we come to know Him intimately we will be enabled to say, "My flesh longeth for thee" (Psalm 63:1).

Then – we will find time for God because we love to be with Him, to hold daily trysts with Him.

Perhaps you are asking, "What is the relationship of the Holy Spirit to prayer? If we are to walk and talk with the Holy Spirit, why is prayer to the Father necessary?" To answer the last question we recall the life of the Lord Jesus. Although He was filled with the Spirit, He frequently spent whole nights in prayer to His Father and it was His habit to arise early to pray. Clearly the filling of the Spirit in no way rules out the need for communion with the Father.

As it was the ministry of the Spirit to bring us to faith, so He is the Fountain of true prayer. As Paul wrote, "God hath sent forth the Spirit of his Son into your hearts, crying, Abba, Father" (Galatians 4:6, Romans 8:15-16).

Since as disciples we are to walk in the Spirit, so all of our actions, whether we classify them as spiritual or natural, religious or secular, are to be empowered by the same Spirit. He is our Power, too, for prayer. We are to "pray in the Holy Spirit" (Ephesians 6:18, Jude 20).

What does this phrase mean? It refers to prayer that flows from a life controlled or filled by the Spirit of God. Such prayer is not asked "amiss, that ye may consume it upon your lusts" (James 4:3). As we pray, walking in the power and presence of the Spirit, we "shall not fulfil the lust of the flesh" in our praying; we shall be praying in keeping with the character of the *Holy* Spirit.

In prayer, as in all other areas, we should be ever-learning.

True satisfaction in the Christian life without prayer is impossible. Most followers know this. And we have all fought to make our prayer lives what we felt they ought to be, something vital and pulsating with life.

But repeatedly we have found that something was missing. We mouthed words, we spoke, but somehow God seemed a long way off. We speak of different kinds of prayer: praise, adoration, asking for things, confession, intercession, *but what is prayer?*

Simply and broadly, prayer is man communicating with God. The exchange may be audible or silent but it is a two-way street. It is not man talking his problems over with himself. Our simple definition suggests several thoughts which may serve as guidelines for an effective and a meaningful prayer life.

1. *Begin your times of prayer with thanksgiving and praise.* This, incidentally, is how you greet your friends. "Hello John. Say, it's great to see you again. I've missed our little chats from time to time." You are, in this common expression, saying, "Thanks for the privilege of knowing you. It has been, and is, a worthwhile relationship."

The Bible puts it this way: "Enter into his gates with thanksgiving, and into his courts with praise: be thankful unto him, and bless his name." If God is, and we've already acknowledged that in becoming Christians, then He is worthy of praise.

In this connection, do not make the error of thinking God must be approached by protocol, red-tape, or religious formulas sanctioned by the church. What kind of friend insists that you always come to him in a predetermined, verbal straightjacket? God is not like that.

2. *Be honest enough to admit it if you have wronged God or man.* It takes some inner excuse-making to converse freely with a person about whom you have gossiped or whom you have wronged in any way. And when a person seeks to approach God with a soiled mind it is sacrilege. And downright foolishness too. Shall a man fool God? As Huck Finn said, "You can't pray a lie – I found that out." Of all masquerades, a holy masquerade is the most detestable.

The Bible puts it this way: "Who shall ascend into the hill of the Lord? or who shall stand in his holy place? *He that hath clean hands, and a pure heart. . . .*" (Psalm 24:3,4).

In another place the Psalmist wrote, "If I regard iniquity in my heart, the Lord will not hear me" (Psalm 66:18). If there is known sin in our lives it should be confessed at once, that our prayers and fellowship be not hindered. Our final acceptance with God and our access into His presence is based on our position in Christ, on His righteousness, not ours. But we have a responsibility to "cleanse ourselves" by confession (II Corinthians 7:1; James 4:8; Psalm 24:3,4).

DON'T HURRY

3. *Pray slowly and thoughtfully but not fearfully.*

A disciple cannot hurry his prayers. This guideline forms the basis of our emphasis on taking time to *be Christians.* We must pray slowly and thoughtfully if we wish to pray effectively. Of course, as we have stressed earlier, God does not expect us to approach Him with fear and trembling; we should not write books when we pray. We should just form the habit of thinking before we speak to God.

Hurried prayers, said habitually and frequently, are one of the serious symptoms of a religious life which neglects God and substitutes in His place religious activity, cliches, taboos, and adherence to shibboleths and esoteric jargon. In other words, the life and language of the "saints" often provides a smoke screen hiding the absence of spiritual reality.

At night, we ready ourselves for bed, kneel, and say, "O God, bless our pastor, his family, and the people in our church, and our missionaries. Help me to be a better Christian. Amen." And then we climb in bed.

The next morning we get up as late as possible, eat a hurried breakfast, look at the clock, and say to the Lord, "You know I don't have much time this morning, but You know how much I love You. I want to walk with You today, so guide me, I'll do my best. Amen."

Many Christians live on such a treadmill. We would do well to slow down; to take more time for prayer, Bible reading, and meditation. If we hope to pray fervently we will have to learn to pray thoughtfully.

When we speak of God as our "Father" or "Almighty God" or "Merciful God" we need to let our little minds grasp the great truth we have spoken. It would profit most of us if we would take time to reflect on, or even write out, our prayers. This would help us grasp the meaning and significance of communicating with an All-knowing God.

When God called to Moses out of the burning bush, He told him "Draw not nigh hither: put off thy shoes from off thy feet, for the place whereon thou standest is holy ground." As Christians the very Spirit of God dwells within us, but this fact in no way grants us the right to approach God frivolously.

4. *When you talk with God, don't forget to listen.* Suppose you pray, "Search me O God." If you really mean this, then you should be quiet (stop talking) and wait. Obviously you can't pray this prayer sincerely and then immediately say, "And bless the missionaries in Africa." It is impolite to ask a question and then not let the person you addressed give you a reply.

WAIT FOR AN ANSWER

It has been my experience that if you pray this prayer and wait quietly and patiently, emptying your mind of other thoughts of the day's activities, God will bring verses or impressions to your mind. In most cases it will be painfully clear what He wants you to know. God will tell you what's wrong – if anything. He also will encourage, comfort, warn, rebuke or inspire you as He sees your need.

God cannot minister to you in this way unless you take time to be with Him – and to listen. The emotional and spiritual well-being that only God can provide is yours every day of your life, and it's free.

We read in James that "the effectual, fervent prayer of a *righteous* man availeth much." We shall, as Christians, maintain a righteous walk with God by allowing no unconfessed sin in our lives and by asking God to search us daily to see if there be any wicked way in us. But this is not the whole answer. The verse also says, "effectual, fervent prayer."

How can our prayers be fervent? I believe that if we will add *time* to our praying, add *thoughtfulness* to our conversation with God, and will add *listening* to our prayer time, our prayers will become more fervent and more meaningful to us and to God.

5. *When you pray, pray broadly, "telling God every detail of your needs"* (Philippians 4:6, Phillips). We read in Philippians 4:6 "Be careful for nothing"; (or as one translation puts it 'Have no anxiety about anything') "but in everything by prayer and supplication with thanksgiving let your requests be made known unto God." Now if this means anything, it means that Christians should not neglect anything, any need, any area of life, when they pray. Truly "we have not because we ask not."

If Christian couples would learn to bring seemingly petty disagreements, resentments, doubts, and other marital maladjustments to God daily in prayer there would be less divorce among believers, and fewer unhappy Christians. (See John 16:24.)

What then should we pray about? First of all, and every day, we should pray for the renewal of our inner man (II Corinthians 4:16). Our concern for continual spiritual development should show itself daily. If we are not growing spiritually day by day then we are sick. If we are satisfied with our spiritual state, then we are sick. Sick Christians are not happy Christians.

Married men should pray daily for their wives. If you

feel that your wife's spiritual life is at low tide, ask yourself if you've been praying for her. If you haven't you can hardly expect too much. Put her on your list, right after your own name. Wives, too, should pray for their husbands.

Parents should pray for their children individually. Each of your children are different, and you certainly should know enough about their personal characteristics and needs to pray with wisdom. This goes back to praying slowly and thoughtfully.

You should survey in your mind little Susie's daily conduct. Does she have trouble getting to school? Do other children tease her? If so, does it upset her unduly? If so, how can you help her with this problem? What does the Lord want you to do to help her? This is the time to pray and wait!

He might suggest you need to read a book on guiding children through the storms and calms of growing up. However, if you could spend all of your time researching the answers to domestic questions, you would still need to depend on Almighty God for wisdom each day.

You may think that such specific prayers are ridiculous but God says "in every thing." If we do not come to Him, we must rely on our own strength and knowledge and this often leads to more anxiety and frustration because we "are not sufficient of ourselves to think anything of ourselves, but our sufficiency is of God" (II Corinthians 3:5).

Surely we should pray for the non-Christians we know and for the Christians we know who are not walking joyfully with the Lord. But keep in mind when praying to ask God what He would have you do; He may want to use *you* to reach the person you are praying for at the time. He will show you what to do – if you ask.

Missionaries, Sunday school pupils and teachers, the pastor, these are a few of the persons who merit and need our intercession. Of course such intercession takes time and interest; and this leads us back to praying for our own spiritual life.

POWER TO PRAY

You cannot be a happy and fruitful Christian if you do not maintain a consistent and enjoyable prayer life. But, strange as it seems, you do not have the power in yourself to pray regularly, or even to desire to pray.

This makes your relationship to the Bible, prayer, and walking with the Lord a matter of *need.* Your needs should be made a matter of prayer. You'll find that if you begin praying about having a daily time with the Lord and His Word, a period of fervent prayer, it will become more and more a habit and not a duty. Ask God to sprinkle your devotional time with blessings, to meet with you in a real way – *and He will do it.*

6. *As you talk with God daily, learn to pray systematically, but don't be a slave to system.* It seems that order pervades the universe. Even our earthly bodies function systematically. We need to eat and sleep regularly. Most Americans eat three meals a day. With some, eating is such a habit that they eat three meals whether they are hungry or not: they might be called slaves to the system.

Certainly we should maintain a continuing attitude of turning to God moment by moment of every day. This is praying without ceasing. But in our stated times of prayer we need some sort of order. How you do this is a personal matter and it will vary from person to person.

A PRAYER LIST

A prayer list for each day of the week can be a great help. With so many things to pray about and so many deserving prayerful consideration, if you do not write them down you will simply forget to pray. Having a list for each day will add substance and order to your praying. Beyond this it can afford variety. The seven sheets of paper can be mixed up occasionally at the beginning of the week. Remember there are solid scriptural grounds for regular times of prayer (Psalm 119:164; Daniel 6:10 and Matthew 14:23). Let us pray regularly.

If we will determine by God's power (the only power we have for spiritual exercise) to pray systematically and broadly, our ministry of prayer will have a strong and broad influence. If we pray slowly and thoughtfully, with a listening ear, our prayer life will be relevant to our daily living, and it will possess the fervency and joy that marks effective prayer.

Speaking of joy and fervency, however, does not mean that at all times and under all circumstances, the believer will experience these emotions. What about the valleys in our Christian walk? Are they part of God's plan, too?

10

Shall We Have . . .

VICTORIES WITHOUT DEFEATS?

Spiritual reality includes the ups and the downs of Christian living. It views defeats and victories, sighs and songs, as necessary and helpful aspects of spiritual growth.

Is there a magical formula, known only to a select few, which can give Christians moment-by-moment triumph *all the time?* Or do all Christians have days when they are literally "under the circumstances"?

When the average layman listens to evangelists or spiritual life speakers, he is often led to conclude that they have found *the answer.* These teachers frequently stress the glorious and exciting experiences of Christian living. Overselling their view in glowing terms they foster the everything-is-thrilling-and-joyful-all-of-the-time concept of spiritual reality.

Mesmerized by this unrealistic and unscriptural theory, Mr. Christian measures his own "sometimes up, sometimes down" experience and asks himself, "What is wrong with my Christian life? Why can't I live on the mountaintop as he (the spiritual life speaker) does?"

The fact is – he doesn't. At least not every second of every minute of every hour of every day. But in his spoken messages he often, for some reason, soft-pedals his own defeats, failures, and doubts.

To offset this exaggerated, blue-sky approach another extreme theory of spiritual reality has invaded the church. Tragically, instead of finding some middle ground between fact and feeling, revelation and reality, it goes to the other extreme and emphasizes the danger of emotions in the Christian life.

To what extent should one's emotions be shunned as valid thermometers of true spiritual living? Can Christians experience a real, heartfelt walk with the living God? Shall we extol the thrills and deny the sighs – or – must we cast all feelings into outer darkness as broken thermometers?

BEWARE EMOTIONS?

The current de-emphasis on emotions pops up everywhere. In magazines, books, from the pulpit, at spiritual life conferences, etc. Its shibboleth is "We walk by faith – not feelings."

The Bible, however, does not describe the Christian life in such terms. We do read in II Corinthians 5:7, "We walk by faith, not by sight." This reference does not, however, deny feelings a place in the Christian life – it merely affirms that our *living* faith operates with things invisible and eternal. As the apostle says earlier, "we look not at the things which are seen, but at the things which are not seen" (II Corinthians 4:18). But we do *look!*

The Apostle Peter puts faith, feeling, and sight in the correct perspective in these words, "Whom having not seen, ye *love;* in whom, though now ye see him not, yet believing, ye *rejoice* with *joy unspeakable* and full of glory" (I Peter 1:8).

This verse illustrates dozens of Biblical passages which, without apology, stress strong emotional tones. Notice it has a clear emotional ring. "Joy unspeakable!" Joy is a positive, action emotion. It throbs with feeling; it is not neutral. Here it is the result of the process of continuing faith in the invisible One. This living faith produces "Joy unspeakable and full of glory."

To soft-pedal this thrilling experiential truth is just as dangerous as presenting it as the moment-by-moment-every-second experience of some "select" saints. The New Testament presents a balanced picture of spiritual reality. We rejoice and we weep. We experience the joys of victory and the sorrows of defeat. Sometimes we complain; at other times we accept things as from the hand of a loving Father. Gradually we grow toward maturity. But never absolute perfection. We travel to higher ground, ever susceptible to slipping back; sometimes able to help others; at other times in great need of help. Always learning more about the ways of God; too frequently having to relearn.

But our schooling occurs in the sphere of a personal, emotional relationship with a loving Father. A Father who loved us so much that "He gave (sacrificed) his only begotten Son." And this same Son of heaven says that the greatest commandment is "Thou shalt love the Lord thy God with all thy heart, and with all thy soul, and with all thy mind" (Matthew 22:37).

Such extreme, all-consuming love involves one's mind and emotions to the very roots of his being. To love God is to become emotionally – yes, intimately – involved with Him.

DEAD FAITH IN A DEAD GOD

To take emotions out of divine love makes God a concept – not a Person. To divest man's response to God, and His love, of genuine emotions makes man's encounters with God strictly mental reactions to a doctrine – not a walk with the *living* God. Either approach can lead to a dead faith in a dead God. Divine love and the human response is both rational and emotional; objective and subjective; fact and feeling.

Jesus spoke of this love-relationship in these words: "He that hath my commandments, and keepeth them, he it is that loveth me: and he that loveth me shall be *loved* of my Father, and I will *love* him, and *will manifest myself to him.*

"Judas saith unto him, not Iscariot, 'Lord, how is it that thou wilt manifest thyself unto us, and not unto the world?'

"Jesus answered and said unto him, 'If a man love me, he will keep my words: and my Father will love him, and *we will come unto him and make our abode* with him'" (John 14:21-23).

Now, how did the Father and the Son plan to make their abode with the believer? And how does Jesus manifest Himself to the believer?

By another Person – the Holy Spirit. He was sent to testify of Christ. He takes the truths of the Father and shows them to the believer (John 16:13-15). And this teaching ministry is a Person-to-person relationship. The Holy Spirit is not a deaf-mute; He hears and He speaks to the listening ear.

Most believers know that the Spirit dwells in their hearts; far fewer know Him personally, recognize His voice, or experience "the communion of the Holy Ghost" (II Corinthians 13:14).

The "fellowship of the Spirit" (Philippians 2:1) and "joy in the Holy Ghost" are not "extras" added to bolster the weak saints who, motivated by lack of faith, seek the conscious presence of God in their experiences; these experiences constitute the normal life of the yielded believer. But this normal life is not all joy, victory and mountaintops; it also includes sorrow, defeat and valleys.

The positive emotions, of course, can prevail during our trials. But we tend to watch the high waves of adversity instead of resting on the undercurrents of joy.

GOD'S TOUCH IN THE DARKNESS

As we learn to "count it all joy when we fall into divers temptations" (James 1:2), we begin by faith to feel God's gentle touch in the darkness. As we exercise patience under trial, we become mature. We come to see God in the midst of our storm. We know He is in control. We sense that God's hand is always there: guiding, controlling, tempering Satan's blows (or our own indiscretions), "not allowing us to be tempted above that we are able," and making "a way of escape." Thus, even as we shed tears, we can rejoice that "He doeth all things well."

Sometimes, however, instead of rejoicing in tribulation, we rebel – in thought, word, or deed. Thus, sin enters our conscious experience. Drawn away by our own lust, we fail to take the way of escape provided. And with sin, comes another host of feelings: defiance, chagrin, remorse, contrition, repentance, confession, and the relief and joy of forgiveness.

Now it is true that some Christians react excessively within the normal emotional pattern of Christian living. But the over-reaction of some should not be met with a policy of pre-meditated underreaction, particularly in an age of depersonalization. The unfeeling Christian is as much a stunted child as the excessively emotional believer; neither is healthy.

The other extreme, the blue-sky, ever victorious theory of spiritual reality, makes it difficult for Christians to recognize God in the routines of everyday life. Much of life is humdrum unless, as we walk in fellowship with the Spirit, we consider our every act or thought as worship, as "done heartily in the name of the Lord Jesus" (Colossians 3:17,23).

In this light it is possible to be "singing and making melody in your heart to the Lord" (Ephesians 5:19) while doing the dishes, writing executive reports, or whatever.

Now and then there will be high spots, victories over ourselves or our circumstances; we will also experience defeats – these too, are a vital part of Christian living, an honest-to-goodness fact of spiritual reality. The man who speaks of advances and victories and never mentions the setbacks and defeats is trimming spiritual reality to fit his preconceived pattern or doctrine. There are defeats, abasements, and times when the overflowing life is listless, calm, and even foul.

In extolling the victorious life, we must make clear the fact and value of defeats. When asserting the danger of trusting one's emotions, we must carefully preserve the richness and fulness of Christian experience. In exorcising Demon Emotion we run the risk of throwing out the baby with the bath water, of stripping Christianity of emotional reality.

The followers of God in all ages have moved up and down the emotional scale while walking by faith: mountaintop and valley experiences, the height of joy and the depths of despair, the exultation of victory and the sighs of defeat. Moses, Isaiah, Jeremiah, David, Peter and Paul all had their spiritual-emotional ups and downs.

And so will we.

They are part of God's plan to conform us to the image of His Son. But "we know that *all* things work together for good to them that love God . . . " (Romans 8:28).

Yes, defeats and victories are part of "life in the Spirit." But what are some other results of His blessed control?

THE RESULTS OF "LIFE" IN THE SPIRIT

To be filled, consciously controlled and empowered, by the Spirit, leads the believer to "walk in the Spirit." The

Spirit becomes his "sphere" of living and this atmosphere or Pneumasphere is capable of description. As the believer's entire life is "enveloped" in the Spirit, basic inherent changes take place gradually.

The Bible speaks of this as our being "changed into the same image of the Lord from glory to glory, even as by the Spirit of the Lord" (II Corinthians 3:18). Or, to put it in other words, the fruit of the Spirit is produced in our lives. We will mention two basic changes born of the Spirit.

First, positive changes will take place in the believer's attitudes. His "interior" life will be actively growing in the graces of Christ or the fruit of the Spirit. Daily conduct at home and at work will become increasingly controlled by the Spirit and the Word. This growth is not merely the result of passive yielding; it also involves diligent cultivation and irrigation. In the words of Peter you are to "do your utmost from your side, and see that your faith carries with it real goodness of life. Your goodness must be accompanied by knowledge, your knowledge by self-control, your self-control by the ability to endure. Your endurance too must always be accompanied by devotion to God; that in turn must have in it the quality of brotherliness, and your brotherliness, must lead on to Christian love" (II Peter 1:5-7 Phillips).

Spiritual growth or "health" arises as the believer walks in the Spirit's fulness. Thus as the believer performs, voluntarily and regularly, the exercises of spiritual life and takes the time and trouble to keep himself spiritually fit, his life changes.

The negative aspect of spiritual growth involves the development of the attitude of our Lord, "Thou hast loved righteousness, and hated iniquity" (Hebrews 1:9). As the Spirit reigns in our lives, this attitude grows in depth and breadth. This elimination of weeds, however, is not an automatic result of yielding. We are *told to* "mortify the deeds of the body."

So Paul writes, "But if . . . you cut the nerve of your instinctive actions *by obeying the Spirit,* you are on the way to real living" (Romans 8:13). Or, if you "Walk in the Spirit, . . . ye shall not fulfill the lust of the flesh" (Galatians 5:16).

Thus, true spiritual living has at least three characteristics:

1. It involves conscious, moment-by-moment acknowledgment and obedience to the Word of the Spirit in our lives. The Bible is the Word of the Spirit.

2. It sees us actively and passively (yielding and yielded) engaged in cultivating the positive virtues of Christ.

3. It includes our own God-induced pruning, weed-destroying efforts of putting to death the sins of the flesh – whatever does not conform to the character and will of God as revealed in His Word.

This book attempts to answer, in part, *how* we can work together with God the Holy Spirit who "works in us both to will and to do of his good pleasure" (Philippians 2:13).

But what can we expect as we seek to "follow after the Spirit"? Again, no one simple answer will apply to all cases. As every human has a mental age differing from his chronological age – so every believer has a spiritual age different from his spiritual-chronological age. All believers are at a different level of spiritual maturity. Once a believer is completely controlled by the Spirit, he will move on to a greater and fuller maturity. And this maturity reaches its ultimate when we will be made into the likeness of Christ.

THE VIRTUE OF LOVE

In addition to the variable we call spiritual growth, every disciple is at a different level of maturity in any given virtue. Take love as an example. Believers are told "to increase and abound in love one toward another" (I Thessalonians 3:12).

But from what point are we to abound or increase? Our present level of maturity.

You see "the fruit of the Spirit is love." But the Spirit's fruit is not a characteristic or attribute handed to us on a silver platter fully grown, nor is it ours in experience by virtue of our "position in Christ." It grows or develops *in* us and *by* us as we consciously walk in the Spirit's fulness.

Some Christians have not been able to love people with dark skin. Their love needs to grow and include all of their "neighbors" – regardless of their race or national origin! Others fail to love believers who disagree doctrinally with their position or creed in *every* detail. Their love is limited by their personal creed. This is not "loving in the truth."

The disciples met such a man and forbade him to cast out demons because he didn't walk with the disciples. Jesus said, "Forbid him not: for there is no man which shall do a miracle in my name, that can lightly speak evil of me. For he that is not against us is on our part" (Mark 9:38).

THE NOURISHMENT OF LOVE

But how can the love of God be increased in us? And what is our part in the process? Certainly it includes passively and actively yielding moment by moment to the Spirit's voice. How shall I determine the Spirit's will? His will is the Word of God of which He is the Author. To know His Word and keep it is to grow in love. The Apostle of love puts if in these words: "Whoso keepeth his word, in him verily is the love of God perfected. . . ." And "This is the love of God, that we keep his commandments" (I John 2:5; 5:3).

LOVE IN YOUR EVERYDAY LIFE

Now let's go back to the "everyday" aspect of life in the Spirit. The Bible teaches that followers of God in all ages have communed with God through words. God has been speaking to men, in one way or another, day by day, since the days of Adam. But is He speaking today, whatever the date you are reading this?

Yes, He is.

And how? In several different ways but chiefly by His Spirit through His Word. And you have the thrilling privilege of listening to Him daily! And by listening and obeying His voice your love will be perfected.

Let the truth of this fact grip your heart. *God–Almighty God, Creator and Upholder of the universe–wants to commune, speak, converse with you every day of your life.*

The tragic truth is that thousands of Christians daily spurn His gracious invitation. They take a raincheck and glibly say, "I will return another day." Regardless of the excuse offered, such neglect leads to spiritual weakness and bondage to sin. Jesus said, "If ye *continue* in my word, *then* are ye my disciples indeed; and ye shall know the truth, and the truth shall make you free" (John 8:31ff).

The Test of Love

To say, "I love the Lord," and not obey the commandments to continue in His Word shows that our love is deficient. Our Master said, "If ye love me, keep my commandments" (John 14:15). He added later, "If a man love me, he will keep my words" (John 14:23). It follows then that a true love for Christ manifests itself in our lives in obedience to His Word. A feigned love neglects His Word. That's what the Lord meant when He said, "He that loveth me *not* keepeth not my sayings" (John 14:24).

Where do you stand?

Do you *daily* meditate, study, learn, observe, keep, follow His commandments and words?

No hedging or excuses!

Either you regularly show your love for God in this way or you do not! Either you are a friend of Christ and are continuing in His Word or you neglect His Word and . . . . It is not difficult to discover if you spend time daily in the Word. Just look back over the past week or month. Did you or did you not?

Attending Sunday school, church, and prayer meeting, does not equal continuing in His Word. These are necessary means of grace but are not sufficient for a walk in the Spirit. As Christ learned obedience to the Father's commandments (words) and lived in His love, so are we to obey and live. As the Master said, "If ye keep my commandments, ye shall abide in my love; even as I have kept my Father's commandments, and abide in His love . . . Ye are my friends, *if* ye do whatsoever I command you" (John 15:10, 14).

The Anatomy of Love

Love for Christ is not a vague feeling, although it includes emotion. It is not mere gratitude, though we are genuinely grateful to Christ for redemption. Love for Christ does not originate *in* you; you love Christ because He first loved you. You cannot continue to love Him apart from the presence and power of the Holy Spirit.

We have spoken of the "nourishment of love." How is love in us to be nourished? It will grow as we spend time in the presence of God, Who is Love. As His love permeates our being, as we become more intimately acquainted with the One who is Love, we will become more like Him, more loving. Our love for Christ and for men emanates from the Holy Spirit as we walk in His fulness. The fruit of the Spirit is love and "the love of God is shed abroad in our hearts by the Holy Spirit, which is given unto us" (Romans 5:4).

By walking with the Spirit and living in His Word, your daily life, every relationship you have with your wife, your children, fellow workers, church friends – will be baptized, immersed, characterized by love. You will be enabled to "walk in love as Christ also hath loved us" (Ephesians 5:2).

If you know a believer, or a non-believer, whom you do not love, you're out of step with God who loves all men, who is Love, and who commands us to love all men (I Thessalonians 3:12). Your growth in love is being thwarted by disobedience and lying. "If a man say, I love God, and hateth his brother, he is a liar: for he that loveth not his brother whom he hath seen, how can he love God whom he hath not seen" (I John 4:20).

As is evidenced by the Thessalonian passage above and Luke 10:30-37, our love should extend beyond believers to include all men. Our Lord taught that we were to love God wholeheartedly and to love our neighbors as we love ourselves. And who is my neighbor? A lawyer once asked Jesus this question. You'll find His answer in Luke 10:30-37.

As true followers of Christ we are to manifest the fruit of the Spirit. And these virtues will become part of our character as we walk in the Spirit's presence and power. And what are these virtues? They are listed in Galatians 5:22, Romans 14:17, Ephesians 5:9, and II Peter 1:5-7. They are:

Love	Meekness
Joy	Temperance (self-control)
Peace	Righteousness
Longsuffering	Truth
Gentleness	Goodness
Faith (faithfulness)	Virtue (Moral goodness)
Patience	Knowledge
Godliness	Brotherly kindness
Faith	

One result of the Spirit's fulness will be definite, though gradual, growth in these fruits as we work and walk diligently with the Spirit day by day.

The activity of the Spirit in a believer's everyday life will produce a hatred of, and a sensitivity to, sin. As he lives daily in the Word–receiving messages of comfort, rebuke, warning, etc., from the Spirit through His Word– and conforming his life to the truth–he will constantly be observing sin in different areas of his life as he exposes them to the revealing and healing light of the Word. The weeding and hoeing part of the process is the confessing and forsaking of sin by the influence of the Spirit.

This cycle will be repeated many times as the believer's many-faceted, multi-role life is enlightened by the Spirit through the Word. New experiences for which we need divine wisdom, drive us to the Word and will lead to continual learning and growth.

When we resist the Light, "we lie, and do not the truth," our fellowship with Christians and the Lord is jeopardized and the blood of Jesus does not cleanse us from sin. If we continue in life to resist, we will be judged at the judgment seat of Christ for "the things done in the body, according to that he hath done, whether it be good or bad" (II Corinthians 5:10).

"But if we walk in the light, as he is in the light, we have fellowship one with another, and the blood of Jesus Christ his Son cleanseth us from all sin" (I John 1:6,7).

Spiritual growth is stunted and the assurance of salvation is forfeited when we walk in known sin. As walking in the Spirit's fulness, in the Light, means to be a healthy, growing Christian, so walking in the knowledge of sin, in the darkness, means to be a sick, degenerating Christian.

Spiritual growth is the lifetime process of "being conformed" to the character of Christ. We learn obedience by the things we suffer and by our sins. We also learn the nature of compassion and forgiveness.

The Spirit thus leads us to build our value system and personal standards on the Word of God as the Spirit teaches us. Fortunately, He *empowers* us to yield our lives daily to Himself that these values can be translated into personal experience and character.

Another result of the Spirit's fulness is verbal witnessing – sharing our daily discoveries with Christians and non-Christians. This truth is developed in the last chapter.

11

HOW TO ENJOY WITNESSING

"For we cannot but speak the things which we have seen and heard . . . ." Witnessing is the spontaneous sharing with Christians and non-Christians of the realities of our faith and our walk with God. We ought to enjoy witnessing. Every Christian ought to experience the thrill of seeing a friend bow his knee and receive "new life" from God.

Again and again the Apostle Paul speaks of his converts as his joy and rejoicing. The Apostle John rejoices when he hears that his "children" are walking in the truth. Rejoicing, in the New Testament, appears as a result of winning others to faith in Christ; it can be the thrilling adventure of every child of God.

OVERFLOW VERSUS "CANNED" WITNESSING

Far too much of today's witnessing stems from the urge to force our convictions upon others. Knowing the plan of salvation, we pass it out indiscriminately to every unbeliever we meet as if all non-Christians possessed the same spiritual readiness. Thus, the greatest truth of the ages becomes our "party line," our "three-minute commercial." Such artificial, mechanistic, and superficial application of God's remedy for sin to the diseases of men often leads to shallow, superficial decisions to follow Christ.

Every Christian is called to be a witness. But all believers are not qualified. Effective witnessing issues from a meaningful walk with the Spirit of the living God. He is the One who sets our lips aflame with the praises of God. He provides the discernment to gauge the unbeliever's readiness. The disciples witnessed to the things which they had seen and heard – unless we walk in the Spirit and know He is working in our lives our witnessing will be uncertain and lifeless.

Surely any forgiven man can witness to what God has done for him. The stirring testimony, however, indicates that God is at work in our lives today. Often Christians can only testify to something that happened in the past; theirs is a past tense faith. To hear them speak, one might conclude that their God passed away shortly after their salvation.

Powerful witnessing grows out of a healthy relationship with God and His Word. The silence of the saints comes from a mental walk with a doctrinal statement instead of a walk with God. This silence is appallingly evident in Bible-believing churches when a testimony meeting is held. The often long-awaited testimony usually gives thanks to God for salvation – ten, twenty, or thirty years ago.

The Old Testament picture of the man of God shows a believer who meditates night and day on the Word and whose lips continually praise the Lord. The New Testament reveals that the walk in the Spirit leads to a life of verbal praise and testimony. This outflow of divine life, this river of living water, is to be channeled to other people.

WITNESSING TO BELIEVERS

Since every believer has a different spiritual age (irrespective of Bible *knowledge,* degrees, etc.), the more mature Christian can and should be lovingly concerned about the babes. This concern is shown in such admonitions as

> Brethren, if a man be overtaken in a fault, ye which are spiritual, restore such an one in the spirit of meekness; considering thyself, lest thou also be tempted.
>
> Wherefore comfort (exhort) yourselves together, and edify one another, even as also ye do.
>
> Confess your faults one to another, and pray one for another, that ye may be healed . . . Brethren, if any of you do err from the truth, and one convert him; let him know, that he which converteth the sinner from the error of his way shall save a soul from death, and shall hide a multitude of sins.
>
> And let us consider one another to provoke unto love and to good works: . . . exhorting one another . . . (Galatians 6:1; I Thessalonians 5:11; James 5:16, 19-20; Hebrews 10:24,25).

Beyond such direct references to corporate concern, is Paul's commendation of the Thessalonian believers: "Ye were ensamples (examples) to all that believe in Macedonia and Achaia. For from you sounded out the word of the Lord not only in Macedonia and Achaia, but also in every place your faith to Godward is spread abroad. . . ."

Such verbal boldness, frankness, and spiritual honesty are seldom seen today among Christians. In their place we have the "I live the life" attitude, "let's avoid the unpleasant truth and confrontation" policy, and a negatively oriented spiritual pride: "I don't this, I don't that," ad infinitum ad nauseum. We should realize that living a positive, healthy Christian life may have little influence on another Christian who is out of step with God – unless that healthy life includes verbal expressions of praise to God and directed conversation on the sore spot.

I recall spending a pleasant evening with a Christian couple. From the conversation, one might have thought they were the happiest couple in the parish. Yet the next day the couple had separated! What folly to talk and act as if life is rosy when the hidden foundations are crumbling beneath us! A novel that depicts this paradoxical behavior in man is *Holy Masquerade* by Olov Hartman (published by Eerdmans).

Another couple whose spirituality was largely negative faced real marital difficulties because they couldn't agree on breaking a child of the thumb-sucking habit. Phariseeism, whether in ancient garb or a sharkskin suit, is still a substitute for spiritual reality. It hides dead men's bones.

Bible study, church services, prayer meetings, witnessing, church service (working for the Lord), and abstaining from certain worldly amusements are not valid signs of spiritual vitality. By no stretch of standards are they signs of spiritual depth. As normal functions of Christian experience they indicate a degree of conformity to acceptable practices.

If such practices consist in the realm of conscious reality, and possess a measure of meaningfulness, they become actual means of grace. If they are only routine, perfunctory habits, they dull the spiritual senses and lead to a stagnant spiritual state.

Rebuking another brother in love, exhorting one another, admitting our faults one to another, and provoking one another to love and good works should be normal experiences among believers. But do these Biblical "checks and balances" operate today? Now and then and here and there among isolated individuals, but not in many local churches.

In questioning believers, the author finds that many lean upon their admitted inadequacy as an excuse. They say, "Who am I to tell another person how to live?" Or in defense, they point out that Galatians 6:1 says, "Ye that are spiritual, restore such an one." Since they do not profess themselves to be "spiritual," their responsibility apparently ceases. Others indicate uncertainty about what it means to be "spiritual" and thus feel out of order in restoring another brother.

As a result a host of spiritual maladies have diseased the Body of believers in this world. When spiritual health is at a low ebb, ever-present disease germs (unspiritual leaders) take over the body. Many members of the Body function at an anemic spiritual level.

If every member neglects to come to the aid of injured members, the entire body will suffer. As Paul puts it, " . . . the eye cannot say unto the hand, I have no need of thee: nor again the head to the feet, I have no need of you" (I Corinthians 12:21).

In this state, the average believer is a mediocre Christian living far below the New Testament standards. The healthy, overflowing, Spirit-filled Christian is so unusual that he is considered fanatic. The normal Christian has become a misfit.

TAKING THE OFFENSIVE

One hallmark of a spiritual believer is the fruit of his lips. (Naturally, this must be accompanied by inner reality and personal experience.) The rejoicing believer, regardless of the adverse or just peculiar reactions of other Christians, must be praising the Lord all the day long. (Psalm 5:11; 7:17; 9:1,2; 35:28; 40:10; 49:3; 66:8; 71:15,24; 77:12; 96:2; 105:2; 113:3; 119:172; 145:2,11; Ephesians 5:18-19; Colossians 3:16, 17; Hebrews 13:15.)

Certainly we should use discretion in the ministry of our lips so as not to alienate, offend, or cause hard feelings. Sometimes, however, such feelings need to arise before the backslider's heart is cleansed. It is never wise to quench the Spirit of praise if the Spirit is truly leading.

We never know the spiritual age of those around us. Suppose one is disheartened in his or her Christian walk. Our words of praise to God may be used by the Spirit to lift his faith. To a believer living in sin our words may serve as an unintended rebuke.

The Christian out of fellowship will not usually take the initiative in introducing spiritual matters. Unless we take the offensive and bring up the subject, we will be trapped in the vortex of innocuous but useless gabble. The author has found leading questions to be helpful in turning a neutral or negative conversation to positive spiritual channels.

To a lunch hour group one might ask, "What do you think is the key to spiritual power?" Or "What have you found to be the greatest help in your private devotional life?" This question will interest those seeking to grow, encourage those who have faltered, and rebuke those who have given up. I have found that even nominal Christians will discuss spiritual things if someone will open the discussion. Care should be taken to avoid *arguing* about walking with the Lord – of all contention, this would seem to be the most sacriligious (I Peter 3:9-11).

Our words should build up the saints (Ephesians 4:29; 5:19; Colossians 3:16; Romans 14:17; 15:14; I Thessalonians 4:18, 5:11). We should be speaking to one another in psalms and hymns, and spiritual songs, singing and making melody in our hearts to the Lord. Note that such speaking results from being filled with the Spirit and letting the Word (message) of Christ dwell in us richly in all wisdom.

EVANGELISTIC WITNESSING

Witnessing to the lost can be classified in two ways: short range and long range communication. The short and long range refers to time, not distance. Short range suggests those brief moments when our lives touch another's and then we part for life. Such moments may seem inconsequential, yet, "A word in season, how good is it!" The author believes that our lives intertwine with others as part of God's sovereign plan and every casual contact with a spiritually dead person should be used for God (as the Holy Spirit leads, of course, in regard to method, need, and openness.) An act of kindness or a tract about salvation, given or done in the name of Christ and in the power of the Spirit may result in someone's salvation.

A tract given to the right person at the right time can be more powerful than a thousand sermons the tract reader may never hear.

Akin to such spirit-led, offensive spot announcements of the Good News, is the local church's ministry of visitation. I'm thinking of the short-range contacts with relative strangers which we might make by visiting. There is a great need for an "offensive" lay evangelism.

Thousands of Bible-believing churches open their doors, wait for the dead to come in, and lament the dead man's indifference to his spiritual needs. If not so prevalent and serious, such an approach would be comical. Imagine fish leaving their own element because we open a building and label it "A Home for Lost Fish"? We might better close the door and go down to the lakes, streams, and rivers where the fish live.

Much of our outreach today is like building a church in the local cemetery, setting up a loudspeaker and calling the dead to our services. Until local churches will actually visit the realm of the dead and speak the dead man's language, they will fail to get a response.

The same is true of individual believers. We cannot win the game unless we take the ball into the enemy's territory. A team that consistently plays defense and has no offensive will not be a consistent winner. For the past 200 years evangelical and fundamental churches and believers have played with the ball at their end of the field, according to their own rules. As a result, the devil's team – which plays a good offensive *and* defensive game – is winning.

Every believer should appoint himself a one-man visitation team and take the Gospel to strangers in his community. Witnessing demands going; we must play the game of winning the lost on the devil's field – not in our dressing room.

As we walk in the Spirit's fulness, our sense of personal responsibility will grow until He impels us to share our own joyful experiences and the Good News. And even this grace takes a certain amount of raw effort, an act of the will in deciding to set aside an evening or whatever, to visit the dead. Sacrifice is called for: a babysitter must be hired, time must be given, and energy must be expended.

Going is not involved, however, in the final classification of witnessing.

Long-Range Witnessing

In the course of life we regularly rub shoulders with the lost. How can we reach those we know well? Again *language* is a key factor, but just one key. Two others are *time* and *friendship*. We use action and language and time to build friendships. This relationship may last for some time with no explicit reference to God. Yet, as the acquaintance ripens, the lost person will observe a difference in value systems, habits, and standards. The cement of friendship is needed to hold the relationship together.

As the friendship grows, opportunities for discussing spiritual matters will frequently arise. The Spirit-filled believer will use these open doors prayerfully, building line upon line. He will obey Peter's words, "But sanctify the Lord God in your hearts: and be ready always to give an answer to every man that *asketh* you a reason of the hope that is in you with meekness and fear" (I Peter 3:15).

Suppose, however, that an opportunity does not naturally open up for an unusually long time. In these cases the believer who has been seeking and watching for openings must take the initiative. Why? Because you can't win the ball game without getting your hands on the ball! A dead man may never bring up the subject of God.

For example, I am dead to the subject of the civilization of the ancient Etruscans. (I'm so dead to this subject that I had to check the encyclopedia to see if there ever was such a civilization – there was – or if the word I had stored in a back room of my mind referred to a kind of silverware.)

Likewise, a spiritually dead man is sometimes that dead to God. It may be that God is only a word in his memory vocabulary, a word with no specific meaning.

I assure you that if an Etruscan enthusiast waited for me to introduce his great interest we would both drop dead before the dialogue started! Therefore, for the lover of God to wait for the lost to bring up the subject of religion, God, Christ, or whatever, may be to play into the hand of the Enemy. So – at times we take the initiative.

More often than not, however, the unsaved man has a residue of Christian training, a collection of attitudes and prejudices, or a number of perplexing questions that will assert themselves in the course of a normal friendship. Then, by listening and asking questions, the believer can form an idea of the subject's nearness to the kingdom of God (Mark 12:28-34). By perceiving his "believing readiness" we can lead him to faith in the living God.

Witnessing is set forth by the New Testament writers as the overflow of a vital walk with God, the Holy Spirit. The Spirit-filled believer enjoys witnessing. He cannot but speak the things which he has seen and heard.

What is the secret of enjoying the Christian life? It is found in daily all-out surrender to the Holy Spirit and His Word, that the life may be filled with His Spirit.